Machine Learning Enhances Intelligent Network

Charles D. Parra

Abstract

The versatile networking services bring about huge influence on daily living styles while the amount and diversity of services cause high complexity of network systems. The network scale and complexity grow with the increasing infrastructure apparatuses, networking function, networking slices, and underlying architecture evolution. The conventional way is manual administration to maintain the large and complex platform, which makes effective and insightful management troublesome. A feasible and promising scheme is to extract insightful information from largely produced network data. The goal of this thesis is to use learning-based algorithms inspired by machine learning communities to discover valuable knowledge from substantial network data, which directly promotes intelligent management and maintenance. In the thesis, the management and maintenance focus on two schemes: network anomalies detection and root causes localization; critical traffic resource control and optimization.

Firstly, the abundant network data wrap up informative messages but its heterogeneity and perplexity make diagnosis challenging. For unstructured logs, abstract and formatted log templates are extracted to regulate log records. An in-depth analysis framework based on heterogeneous data is proposed in order to detect the occurrence of faults and anomalies. It employs representation learning methods to map unstructured data into numerical features, and fuses the extracted feature for network anomaly and fault detection. The representation learning makes use of word2vec-based embedding technologies for semantic expression.

Next, the fault and anomaly detection solely unveils the occurrence of events while failing to figure out the root causes for useful administration so that the fault localization opens a gate to narrow down the source of systematic anomalies. The extracted features are formed as the anomaly degree coupled with an importance ranking method to highlight the locations of anomalies in network systems. Two types of ranking modes are instantiated by PageRank and operation errors for jointly highlighting latent issue of locations.

Besides the fault and anomaly detection, network traffic engineering deals with network communication and computation resource to optimize data traffic transferring efficiency. Especially when network traffic are constrained with communication conditions, a pro-active path planning scheme is helpful for efficient traffic controlling actions. Then a learning-based traffic planning algorithm is proposed based on sequence-to-sequence model to discover hidden reasonable paths from abundant traffic history data over the Software Defined Network architecture.

Finally, traffic engineering merely based on empirical data is likely to result in stale and sub-optimal solutions, even ending up with worse situations. A resilient mechanism is required to adapt network flows based on context into a dynamic environment. Thus, a reinforcement learning-based scheme is put forward for dynamic data forwarding considering network resource status, which explicitly presents a promising performance improvement.

In the end, the proposed anomaly processing framework strengthens the analysis and diagnosis for network system administrators through synthesized fault detection and root cause localization. The learning-based traffic engineering stimulates networking flow management via experienced data and further shows a promising direction of flexible traffic adjustment for ever-changing environments.

List of Abbreviations

AI	Artificial Intelligence
ANN	Artificial Neural Network
API	Application Program Interface
AR	Auto Regression
ATM	Asynchronous Transfer Mode
CNN	Convolutional Neural Network
CEGAR	Counterexample Guided Abstraction Refinement
CSI	Channel State Information
DBSCAN	Density-Based Spatial Clustering of Applications with Noise
DBN	Deep Belief Net
DDPG	Deep Deterministic Policy Gradient
DM	Dependency Matrix
DL	Deep Learning
DRL	Deep Reinforcement Learning
EM	Expectation-Maximization
GNU	GNU Is Not Unix
GPU	Graphic Processor Unit
GRU	Gated Recurrent Unit
HMM	Hidden Markov Model
HPC	High Performance Computing
HVFT	High Volume Flexible Time

ICN	Information Centric Networking
i.i.d.	Independent and Identical Distributed
IoT	Internet of Things
IP	Internet Protocol
IPLoM	Iterative Partitioning Log Mining
NDN	Named Data Networking
NLP	Natural Language Processing
NN	Neural Networks
NTF	Non-negative Tensor Factorization
NUM	Network Utility Maximization
MDP	Markov Decision Process
MPLS	Multi-Protocol Label Switching
LCS	Longest Common Subsequence
LSTM	Long Short Term Memory
OCC	One-Class Classification
OSPF	Open Shortest Path First
OSVM	One-class Support Vector Machine
QoE	Quality of Experience
QoS	Quality of Service
RBF	Radial Basis Function
RNN	Recurrent Neural Networks
RL	Reinforcement Learning
RTT	Round Trip Time
SDN	Software Defined Network
SDR	Software Defined Router
SDWN	Software Defined Wireless Network
SIG	Structure-of-Influence Graph

SLCT	Simple Logfile Clustering Tool
SR	Segment Routing
STE	Statistical Template Extraction
TE	Traffic Engineering
TEM	Trace Error Matrix
TF-IDF	Term Frequency–Inverse Document Frequency
VoIP	Voice over Internet Protocol

Table of Contents

List of Figures

List of Tables

Chapter 1

Introduction

1.1 Overview

The emerging versatile networking services [1] has greatly improved daily life styles while making the current Internet environment increasingly hierarchical and complicated. With the advent of novel applications, e.g., video streaming, VoIP and etc., the global servicing policy demands network system rapid scaling and being compatible with stale-fashioned facilities. It imposes massive stress on its effective management. Human force-based administration inevitably exposes of its serious low-efficiency defect due to the complexity raised by large-scale distributed network systems. The distributed and paralleled architecture can easily disorder the informative records by concurrent executions and isolate one integrated function as separated parts.

A network management system dedicates to a productive networking environment with stable fundamental mechanisms [2]. It is usually via its core functions, e.g., monitoring, analysis, alerting and etc., to provide reliable and elastic networking services. In order to maintain smooth operation status and provide high quality services, the networking anomaly and fault analysis becomes one of the primary task of benign network management, which has drawn substantial attention to researchers [3, 4]. It has become unrealistic and wasteful to manually discover useful and hidden clues from intensely intersected histories. Because of costly manual recognition, the automation of analysis and processing is a straightforward approach to gain overwhelmingly efficient performance of anomaly detection.

The anomaly and fault analysis focuses on abnormal networking behaviors detection and root cause localization [5] through elaborating dissection of system intrinsic knowledge and dynamic status data. It is of special significance since one serious incident occurrence has a large change to result in heavy performance reduction, further serious local malfunction and even a catastrophic global collapse. There is no doubt that in large-scale distributed networking environment, application-oriented manual analysis with ad-hoc auxiliary toolkits and expertise fails to match the speed of the ever-changing system utility. The common wisdom to relieve the processing pressure is to take full advantage of machine status record data with state-of-the-art analysis automation enabled by data mining and machine learning algorithms [2, 6]. The existing data-driven efforts endeavor to build models based on specific applications to perceive the implicit value of data. Although notable performance has been reached, there still lacks a compatible regulation to fuse multiple data sources and synthesize a joint data representation from the perspective of broader scenarios. One core intention of this thesis is to concentrate on anomaly and fault analysis under the large-scale distributed network circumstance.

Technically, the anomaly and fault analysis is a reactive process to networking management, since the analyzer awaits status records data and discovers information of special interest. To pro-actively keep benign operation state of a system, the adaptive network resource management mechanism is required, such as Traffic Engineering. Traffic Engineering (TE) is crucial for enhancing the utility and performance of networks in the era of big data [7, 8]. It has been a hot topic in recent research trend [7–11], due to the increasing demands on dynamic network maintenance, management and Quality-of-Service (QoS) guarantee [8]. Increasing network service demands generate considerable data, while the data entail informative patterns describing the features and in turn will benefit the learning-based methods. This thesis will consider the serious challenges of applications for large-scale and complex network traffic engineering.

1.2   Network Environment and Scenarios

Generally, the network management solution targets at a complex, highly correlated and inconsistent background environment, as shown in Fig. 1.1. As generalizing to broader applications, the work flow can be separated into three planes, networking infrastructure plane, data collection and retrieval plane, and general purpose analysis plane. From Fig. 1.1, the first networking plane consists of infrastructures and active apparatuses, upon which key status and operation data collectors are embedded and deployed. On the left side, users connect to the Internet via portable and wired desktop-based devices, where user access, queries and reports are retrieved through data collection interfaces. Similarly, on the right side, service providers respond to users with complete results, where system execution sequences are stored in service behavior data warehouse. As interaction middle layer, network base station, routers, switches and etc., couple the two sides as a complete network connection process, where communication traces are tracked and retrieved into communication tracing warehouse. Within the data retrieval plane, data warehouses are supposed to be maintained uniformly by off-the-shelf database techniques to keep efficiency of subsequent analysis access.

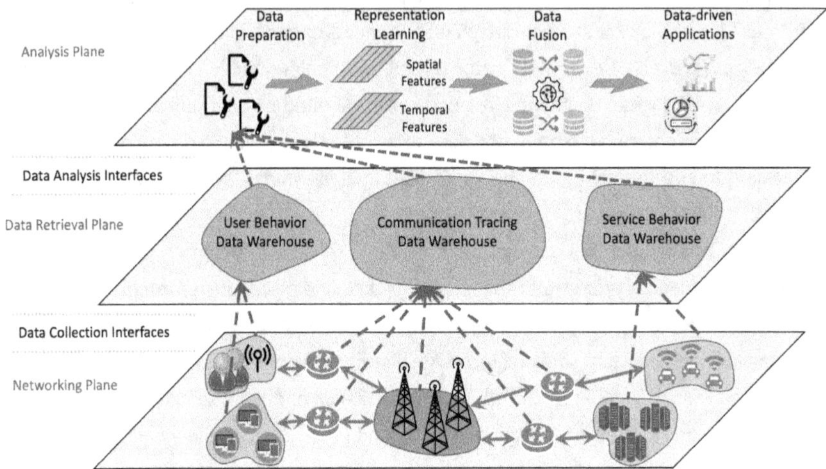

Fig. 1.1 Data-driven Work Flow in Large-scale Distributed Network.

The separated planes unambiguously illustrates a universal purpose analysis architecture from underlying meta-data collection through customized data storage and preparation to analysis engine. Based on the current underlying stale and novel collection mechanisms, data obtained are organized in terms of various formats and are stored in easy-access database for regular retrieval. As aforementioned, current efforts are inclined to either base on an empirical deterministic model or expert experiences, which weakens the generalization capacity. The top layer in Fig. 1.1 displays an overview of potential streaming pipeline-like work flow consisting of extracting spatial-temporal characteristics and incorporating data heterogeneity for the downstream insightful analysis and decision tasks.

1.3 Motivation

1.3.1 Intelligent Anomaly and Fault Analysis

The scale of network environment, for example, the typical micro-services architecture [12–15], can easily hide small-size troubles with ambiguous symptoms in various locations and the informative data can flood into downstream tasks. One of the crucial tasks is anomaly and fault deep analysis consisting of occurrence detection and root localization [16], which guarantees reliability and robustness of a system. To accomplish this task, informative messages are indispensable and produced endlessly while excessive data can in turn flood into analyzers preventing immediate issue discovery and settlement. The information is likely to be temporal in text-formed logs and time-series, or spatial in tracing records and locations, which can be heavily twisted and entangled. As such, intelligent and fast processing mechanisms are in urgent need to obtain in-depth understanding of implicit attributes to discover latent failures by abundant data.

1.3.2 Traffic Engineering from Hidden Knowledge

Another vital issue in network management is traffic engineering that involves in optimizing the data transferring in network environment. The traffic often appear in a large-scale distributed network system, i.e., the SDN, with controllable switches and routers. When the volume of traffic increases promptly exceeding the growth of apparatuses, the stale-fashioned and locally-optimal traffic engineering will inevitably reduce the performance of networking [10, 11]. On the other hand, substantial event records and trace data are also kept, which probably entails hidden knowledge to globally perceive the complex situation. The knowledge that can be inferred from experiences is able to assist in-depth prediction, planning and decisions to optimize network utility. The processing mechanism driven by knowledge and history data are undoubtedly beneficial to global and adaptive traffic engineering by proactive planning, which leads to data transfer path calculation.

1.4 Challenges

As the complexity of network equipment grows, the amount and perplexity of data increases promptly, which heavily obstructs the efficiency of network management. Here, several challenges are listed but not limited in the following ways:

Knowledge Learning for Anomaly and Fault Analysis:
  Traditional perspective to anomaly analysis is confined to single data source mining and learning, which is inclined to neglect featured clues from other types of data. For instance, the isolated temporal and spatial data analysis loses the correspondence between each other. Furthermore, versatile network components tend to constantly generate its own pre-defined mutually inconsistent information, probably including human-readable text network logs, temporal traffic frames, spatial topology graphs and etc. Though multi-source data analysis is a viable idea to extract joint information from multiple data source, there lacks a universal processing mechanism to deal with

non-uniform data, like time-based sequences and space-based structures. To be specific, sequential logs serve as a prevalent record means for most of network equipments while they are defined as distinctive formats. The seemingly chaotic logs with volatile data variables are not suitable for numerical computing. Though the structural processing can be implemented to some extent, categorical data still prevents semantics analysis to fully understand the implication of logs. That is categorical data lacking numerical representation to fit in the recent advances of machine learning algorithms. Another noteworthy issue is that the simple message combination solely unveils incidents occurrence without useful sources of root causes to guide subsequent maintenance. Apparently, the root causes shall be discovered from heavily twisted and interleaved data without straightforward hints.

Experience Interpretation for Traffic Path Planning

Three serious issues are considered to be heavy influences of traffic path planning. Firstly, the conventional wisdom of traffic path prediction is to consider neighborhood status collected by one single router or switch, which rarely holds global view. Additionally, the traditional switch devices can only perceive local regional and interconnected nodes so that optimization algorithms are prevented from fetching global information. Presumably, the recent advances in Software-Defined Network (SDN) is able to adjust static data traffic schemes into elastic architectures, which separates networking behaviors as pure data transferring and environment-aware decision-making. Secondly, as for decision-making, the traditional ways attempt to formulate strict mathematical models to fully adapt to various situations, however the realistic environments are ever-changing without fixed paradigms so that failing to fit in strict models. Therefore, knowledge learning for flexible decision is required to adapt to shifty physical situations. Thirdly, elastic decision-making will lead to urgent demand of knowledge extraction and interpretation from networking experience data. Nevertheless, massive correlated information are produced accordingly without clear clue of how relevant they are to targeted optimization applications. Furthermore, networking data contain large amount of unstructured and categorical data that fail to be integrated into numerical analysis. As such, adaptive methods should be employed to digest various data and export insightful knowledge accordingly.

1.5 Contributions

This thesis endeavors to tackle large-scale network management issues in terms of network anomalies and faults detection; root causes localization; constrained traffic engineering; and adaptive and flexible traffic engineering. These contributions are summarized as below:

Anomaly and Fault Detection and Localization Scheme:
> The proposal aims at general anomaly and fault detection and localization in the context of micro-services via temporal-spatial joint analysis including representation learning for categorical log data and tracing representation, and via root cause analysis with service importance index.

> Categorical log data are with temporal features from the perspective of sequential log generation. To deal with log data, we firstly propose a recursive partitioning log template extraction algorithm that has competitive performance and achieves faster processing speed. It accomplishes uniformly formating unstructured logs. Secondly, distributed representation-based semantic expressions are proposed for abstract log templates and individual tasks. It transforms categorical data into computable numerical vectors. Spatial data relate to locations of system services and the interactions among themselves. We propose the system service dependency and spatial correlation based on a distributed service-based tracing mechanism with calling duration and frequency. It transforms topological configurations into interpretable numerical representations. To reveal the hidden root causes, we propose a two-stage root cause localization framework through anomaly degree computation based on Deep Learning and a service importance index ranking mechanism based on PageRank. It extracts latent dependency from intrinsic topology.

Experience Learning based Traffic Engineering:
> The proposal is designed to adapt knowledge learning from experience data into constrained networking data transferring path proactive planning.

> History requested networking data are regarded as sequence-based experience for sequences transformation. The planning resembles a sequence construction processing. We therefore propose a sequence-to-sequence based model for constrained forwarding traffic planning, enhanced by the attention mechanism to perceive path context and beam search to avoid local optimal. It captures data forwarding directions and infers available segments. Pure knowledge mining from experience with paired labels is a rigid supervised process, however the physical network is dynamical and unstable, which requires an adaptive planning outline. We accordingly propose a Deep Re-

inforcement Learning based model for constrained forwarding planning to mitigate throughput reduction and for dynamic forwarding strategy based on the previous accessed path. It focuses on elastic routing and forwarding strategies for ever-changing environment.

1.6 Overview of This Thesis

The remainder of this thesis is briefly presented here:

Chapter 2 investigates and categorizes notable research contributions in the sphere of network management with respect to anomaly and fault analysis and traffic engineering. It consists of the traditional statistics-based methods and recent learning-based algorithms for both anomaly analysis and traffic engineering. Additionally, the text-based log template extraction reviews are introduced for log data based anomaly analysis.

Chapter 3 introduces temporal and spatial data joint analysis for anomaly and fault detection through representation learning. The temporal data are system logs that record key status. With proposed segment and partition based template extraction, unstructured logs are converted into abstract forms. The spatial data come from service trace information which genuinely captures the dependency of queries. The heterogeneous temporal and spatial data are semantically vectorized by the representation learning and jointly assist the final samples identification.

Chapter 4 proposes a two-stage analysis scheme for ranking-based root cause localization. The first stage focuses on the anomaly degree inferred from operation logs by fitting a neural sequential model. This process not only attempts to approximate sequential relations in normal conditions but also highlight the most obvious discrepancy between the expectation and practice. At the second state, an importance value is calculated based on the PageRank algorithm and an error tracing matrix is constructed to merge as a synthesized index. The synthesized index is then used to rank the most suspicious service pointing at a specific task.

Chapter 5 introduces the sequence-to-sequence framework from Natural Language Processing into network traffic data fitting. With the strength of attention mechanism and beam search, the data flow forwarding path is well planned under the node location constrains. The model is trained with the path records in two topologies and is deployed in the Mininet Software Defined Network (SDN) emulator to evaluate its feasibility.

Chapter 6 focuses on the adaptive traffic engineering in difference scenarios from the perspective of Reinforcement Learning, which is enhanced by Deep Learning at the same time. For the node constrained application in the GEANT topology, the Deep Q-learning is able to find the optimal constrained node to reduce the throughput loss. For the dynamic path prediction in the 10×10 Grid topology, the Deep Q-learning converges to a stable level that offers the highest throughput for the data transferring requests. The empirical results show the promising direction for the future networking architecture traffic engineering.

Chapter 7 draws the core conclusion of the thesis and introduces several future directions and work.

Chapter 2

Literature Review

When it comes to network management, the common wisdom is an in-depth understanding of a network system and an effective control based on the understanding. It involves five core topics defined by the International Organization for Standardization (ISO) network management model [17], including fault, configuration, accounting, performance, and security management, acronymized as the FCAPS. Specifically, the fault management refers to a series of systematic proactive and reactive behaviors towards network fault occurrence; the configuration management corresponds to core settings that control network devices; accounting management monitors and analyzes the status of all types of users; performance management keeps track of the measurement of networking performance and quality of services; lastly, the security management guarantees legal and safe access to all assets through the authorization and authentication. Centralized and decentralized schemes [18, 19] are successively proposed to improve its utility and capacity. The challenges [19, 20] are constantly increasing because of incremental magnitude and complexity of physical network equipments and structures. Intelligent and cognitive proposals are introduced to make networking available and reliable [1, 5, 20].

In addition to the contributions in academia, many systematic implementations are achieved in practice to conduct pragmatic trials. Three typical trials have gained popularities across industries, from an enterprise-oriented commercial solution, Splunk[1], to an open-sourced components integration, ELK[2], and to a composite management platform, OpenNMS[3]. Splunk has a reputation in commercial IT infrastructure, offering operational and systematic status monitoring and analysis. It is enterprise-oriented and can take input as text-formatted logs, time-series data and other meta-data. The ELK framework, which stands

---

[1] https://www.splunk.com/
[2] https://www.elastic.co/elk-stack
[3] https://www.opennms.com/

for Elasticsearch, Logstash and Kibana, is comprised of three discrete open-sourced projects providing scalable and customizable heterogeneous data digestion. The ELK seamlessly integrates the three data analysis tools for multi-source data parsing by Logstash, indexing and searching by Elasticsearch, and visualizing analysis insights by Kibana. OpenNMS platform is based on community development for distributed and scalable network system management and monitoring. It provides stable and reliable enterprise-level performance for health supervision of networking systems. All three practices have a user-friendly and on demand visualization interface to relieve system administration pressure caused by data flood. Nevertheless, prevalent analysis paradigms with application specific handling lack flexible heterogeneous data analysis capacity. The well-designed systems endeavor to fit in preset data type for general purpose so that they are unable to adaptively and automatically discover unknown structures.

This chapter reviews necessary technical background and relevant literatures of log analysis and application, and network traffic resource management. As the main work is to pursue intelligent network operation and maintenance, the chapter includes two sections, covering background knowledge and recent research advances. The structure is as follows: log analysis for network maintenance is introduced at first, which includes text log data pre-processing, and statistics-based and learning-based network fault detection and localization; in the following, traffic engineering for intelligent network management is presented, which consists of prevalent traditional and deep learning model based research.

2.1 Log Analysis for Network Maintenance

The well known Murphy's law [21] can be stated as "Anything can go wrong, will go wrong" to describe the occurrence of potential negative situations. This indicates that faults and failures could highly frequently happen in modern electronic systems, such as digital computer systems. In order to quickly discover and recover from failures, logging mechanism is commonly embedded to record serious issues and track those severe back to source [22].

Originally, logging module is utilized as a developing probe inserted into key positions for developers to debug and track work-flow [22, 23]. However, the readable textual message somehow gives insight of one system, which promotes operation monitoring and trouble diagnosis [24]. Since recent developments, e.g., microservice-based frameworks [12], are growing increasingly complex, a specific well-designed logging component becomes vital to efficiently detect and localize possible failures. The logging module has been integrated as one of the core functions for high reliability.

In section 2.1.1, log data preprocessing is firstly introduced, followed by statistics-based and learning-based fault detection and localization, in section 2.1.2 and 2.1.3, respectively. In section 2.1.4, Deep Learning based progresses will be insightfully presented as well.

2.1.1　Log data Preprocessing for Analysis

Log preprocessing is the foundation of downstream tasks, as raw log messages are unstructured, disordered and even possibly corrupted [25]. Generally, the downstream analysis of log data, e.g., statistic learning and deep learning, is always inclined to take as input numerical and categorical data, which requires raw log information being cleaned, ordered, and normalized. Especially, when considering statistic learning and machine learning related algorithms, numerical data is preferred, even compulsory. It is clear that in preprocessing, raw logs are supposed to be tailored and transformed.

In general, one log record would consist of two parts: *log head entry* and *log message entry*. In *log head entry*, there exist several segments, e.g., time stamp indicating system time when the particular event taking place, Host name indicating physical machine marks, and severity indicating how serious is the particular event, etc. The detailed segments depend on the operation system where the software is running, but will keep consistent with standard and unified format across all the stored logs. In the meanwhile, *log message entry* is pre-defined manually by developers, which may differ significantly amongst systems, even within one module, as developers in a group may also have distinctive logging standards.

Table 2.1 illustrates a block of raw log message examples generated from IBM BlueGeneL supercomputer [25].

Table 2.1 Raw Log Message Samples Collected in BlueGene/L Supercomputer

LOG HEAD ENTRY	LOG MESSAGE ENTRY
2005-06-05-07.43.29.199690 R35-M0-N1-C:J02-U01 RAS KERNEL INFO	INSTRUCTION CACHE PARITY ERROR CORRECTED
2005-06-05-07.43.29.223683 R35-M1-N9-C:J03-U01 RAS KERNEL INFO	INSTRUCTION CACHE PARITY ERROR CORRECTED
2005-06-07-22.17.51.624699 R03-M0-N7-C:J02-U01 RAS KERNEL INFO	INSTRUCTION CACHE PARITY ERROR CORRECTED
2005-06-07-22.17.51.651067 R06-M1-NC-C:J11-U01 RAS KERNEL INFO	GENERATING CORE.53489
2005-06-07-22.17.51.677398 R06-M1-NC-C:J06-U01 RAS KERNEL INFO	GENERATING CORE.53489
2005-06-07-22.17.51.703324 R06-M1-NC-C:J02-U11 RAS KERNEL INFO	DISABLE STORE GATHERING..................0
2005-06-07-22.17.51.728819 R05-M0-N1-C:J17-U11 RAS KERNEL INFO	CE SYM 2, AT 0X0B85EA80, MASK 0X08
2005-06-07-22.17.51.754779 R05-M0-N1-C:J08-U11 RAS KERNEL INFO	NODE CARD IS NOT FULLY FUNCTIONAL
2005-06-07-22.17.51.784808 R05-M0-N1-C:J08-U01 RAS KERNEL INFO	CE SYM 21, AT 0X110035E0, MASK 0X80
2005-06-07-22.17.51.850973 R14-M1-NF-C:J03-U11 RAS KERNEL INFO	CE SYM 2, AT 0X0B85EA80, MASK 0X08

It is manifest that in Table 2.1, a log record basically consists of two main parts, defined as *Log head entry* and *Log message entry*, respectively. By "log record", some may also consider it as "log entry", therefore the two expressions will be used exchangeably.

There exits formatted log meta-data inside the *Log head entry*, recording event time, event source (host), class, belonging, and severity [26]. The information is usually appended and inserted based on priori experiences which are considered as potential necessities to developers and administrators. With the formatted information, no extra operation but statistical summary and separation would be taken to provide intuitive rough system health trend knowledge.

What always draws administrators' attention is the unstructured *Log message entry*, which is basically written in natural language and contains abundant fragmented clues to system status at one particular time point. The log message style could vary among systems or even inside one large-scale system which is modularly created by several developing groups. Because of the unstructured property and trivial numerical variables, it is difficult to mine coarse-grained and high-level systematic events in the sense of human understanding. In order to form comprehensive systematic execution states, relative work has been done firstly aiming at mining compact, stable and interpretable message representations, also can be called message patterns and templates [27, 26, 28–33]. The common idea across the research is treating log message as two elements, constant expressions and variable values, respectively. The constant expressions are consistent repeating information body, which are usually fixed in the system source code, e.g., message wrapped as constant string-type in "print"-style functions and methods. In contrast, the variable values are reserved entries inside a "print"-style methods, varying based on the incoming specific conditions, e.g., the integer type replacement as "%d". Therefore, the main task has become to construct an abstraction in which the constant entries are kept and the variables are reduced into an substitution such as wild card "*" with the corresponding numbers and positions. The extracted message abstraction is called "template" or "patterns". In this thesis, the two terminologies are used interchangeably.

Table 2.2 Template/Pattern Examples

RAW LOG MESSAGE PART	EXTRACTED PATTERNS
INSTRUCTION CACHE PARITY ERROR CORRECTED	INSTRUCTION CACHE PARITY ERROR CORRECTED
CE SYM 2, AT 0X0B85EA80, MASK 0x08	CE SYM *, AT *, MASK *
GENERATING CORE.53489	GENERATING *
DISABLE STORE GATHERING...................0	DISABLE STORE GATHERING...................0
NODE CARD IS NOT FULLY FUNCTIONAL	NODE CARD IS NOT FULLY FUNCTIONAL

Extraction examples based on Table 2.1 are illustrated in Table2.2. From Table 2.2, five templates are extracted, wherein three of them remain the same as the raw log and the rest two have been reduced to compact style. It is because some raw messages are defined with constant strings to represent a fixed system status. With such compressed format, the downstream task takes the extracted types as input to enable deeper analysis. An empirical evaluation over four prevalent algorithms has been compared in [34, 35], in which running time and parsing accuracy are examined as performance metrics.

Statistics-based template extraction

Kimura et al. proposed a statistical template extraction (STE) method [27] for the afterwards numerical log information tensor factorization by parsing massive log collection without assumption of prior system knowledge. They conjecture that constant terms that are parts of template should occur more frequently than variable terms, and the similar structured information will share the same base template. Two stages are included: scoring and clustering. In the scoring phase, each term score is denoted by the occurrence probability conditioned on occurrence position and the message length.

$$S(term, position, length) = Prob(term|position, length)$$

Here, each *term* is separated by punctuation(usually, by space or tab), the *position* is the term occurrence order within a log message, and the *length* is total term count of one message. As for occurrence position and message length, it is assumed that one template has the invariant count of terms across real log messages and frequent template terms should tend to appear in the same positions with respect to the base template. In the clustering phase, the variable term are removed based on the score. Apparently, the score of frequent template terms are larger than variables, while a simple threshold is not easily determined and may introduce extra noise. Therefore, the DBSCAN [36] (Density-based spatial clustering of applications with noise) algorithm is applied to divide terms into constants and variables. By choosing the density and top terms clusters, the eventual template should keep $\beta * length$ constants, where β is a ratio parameter, $0 < \beta < 1$.

In [29], the author develops a tool called SLCT(Simple Logfile Clustering Tool) to implement the proposed frequent items mining based clustering algorithm, which has very close relationship with the Apriori algorithm [37]. Starting with the Apriori algorithm, it is utilized as association rules learning [38] to mine frequent items or co-occurrence items within a database transaction. Furthermore, the Apriori algorithm will fix a *support* threshold to determine the frequency. Here, the *support* is the count of items or co-occurrence items across the entire transaction records set. Simply put, the Apriori algorithm finds out any frequent items or item associations with the frequency defined by an occurrence count threshold. Unlike the Apriori algorithm, which may incur large memory cost, the SLCT attempts to scan the entire log data as less as possible. The SLCT includes three steps: identifying frequent words; building cluster candidates; and fixing the final cluster representation. Firstly, it defines a *region* as a set of word-level items which are assigned with identical values and multiple attributes. If only one attribute is conveyed in one item, the *region* is also named as *1-region*. Through inspecting log messages line by line, all the

1-regions, namely one *word* with its absolute position inside one log record as the attribute, are recorded with a user specified occurrence value. Secondly, each log message will be scanned once again to detecting if it belongs to any *1-regions*. If once identified as one or more *1-region*, the corresponding one *1-region* or multiple *1-region* combination will be stored in a cluster candidate library as a potential candidate. The last step is to select the well-formatted *1-region* combinations from the candidate library by confirming that all *regions* must equal or exceed a support threshold value.

Similar to [27], the proposed method also makes use of the statistical characteristics of single word entries and the maximum items assumption that those log messages sharing the same templates equal in terms of length. However, Vaarandi et al. claim in [31] that there exists another situation that messages may share the same base template, whereas variables may cross multiple entries. The case is exemplified as strings embedded with spaces and tabs are passed to string placeholders, such as "%s", in system source code. In order to tackle the situation, Vaarandi et al. propose improvement [31], called "LogCluster". In this work, the log messages are firstly treated as the same way as [29]. Opposed to the attributed *1-region* identification, the candidates are stored with flexible position to reserve a placeholder for a variable count summary. The count summary is depicted as $*\{lst, mst\}$, where *lst* and *mst* indicate the least and most occurrence position of variables. By the means, LogCluster is designed to be insensitive to shifting variable positions and flexible log pattern length.

Regardless statistical characteristics, some other research [39, 32] dedicates to gather the longest common subsequence(LCS) to identify sharing intrinsic structure across similar log messages. In [39], not only message part but information header is also considered as parsing objective. The authors propose a metric called *Match Score* to formulate the log extraction process as maximizing an objective function summing all the match scores between a potential pattern and log messages. On top of such definition, the method reduces log messages into pairs and approximate the maximal employing a local search algorithm. Finally, the message template, depicted as *message signature* in [39], is regarded as a sequence of terms that exceeds the half of the cardinality of the candidate group. Contrary to scanning the global log set and operating in batch-style, [32] attempts to gain achievements in streaming-like data set, called Streaming Parser for Event Logs using an LCS (Spell). Instead of maintaining a global template list, the initialized LCSMap list is empty. As the one message is flowed into the parser, the longest common subsequent is computed. The one whose common part is longer than a threshold will be considered as sharing the same underlying template. The final templates are also processed as sequences, in which variables are substituted by wild cards.

Source code-based template extraction

When dealing with a particular system, administrators who have more key knowledge are more familiar with information conveyed in logs. Knowledge based methods assume that researchers have necessary part of log module knowledge to employ heuristics, differing from other parsing solutions [40, 41]. Jiang et al. [40, 41] investigate several approach categories, e.g., Rule-based, Codebook-based and AI-based, and they defined four criteria, namely *interpretability*, *Needed system knowledge*, *required effort*, *Coverage*, to measure the performance and applicability of existing log processing approaches. The assumption is that the source code can be accessed. Their algorithm is based on CCFinder, a source code clone detection tool [42], which utilizes *parameterized token-matching algorithms*. To tackle large-scale log records, the proposed approach includes three steps: *Anonymize*, *Tokenize*, and *Categorize*. Enabled by the prior knowledge, heuristics are applied to abstract variable values in particular positions localized by pre-defined symbols and phrases, such as "=". The heuristics come from the source code analysis, by which the log module confirm to one standard recording style. Secondly, the *Tokenize* step mainly separates the entire dataset into candidate structure clusters, by identifying the length of anonymized log messages. It accepts that the underlying shared templates tend to generate equally long logs. Lastly, from the *Categorize*, candidate clusters are inspected through line by line to discriminate unique format class. Each cluster can be subdivided into unique log type since the remain static terms are not aligned if the candidates fail to share a template. Comparing with the SLCT, the knowledge-based method outperforms it by achieving more than 90% extraction precision and 99% recall.

Partitioning-based template extraction

Through the statistics and knowledge based log parsing method above, some strict assumptions and strong user-specified parameters are required, which limits the feasibility and utility. To avoid unstable parameter setting and prior knowledge requirement, partitioning-based methods prefer to manipulating the log structure to represent the underlying format rather than gathering global information.

In [43], a partitioning-based log key extraction, called LKE, is proposed to deal with system threads and work-flow log events. The extraction consists of four steps: removing obvious variable parameters; raw key clustering; partitioning by groups; fixing the final keys. To remove variable part in log templates, heuristics and empirical rules are applied base on deep understanding of system by setting up regular expressions to shrink apparent variables. It eases the process of subsequent operations. To cluster the intermediate raw log keys, the authors seek to compare log keys by computing a weighted edit distance, which by the general metric definition is Levenshtein distance [44]. The Levenshtein distance initially measures string difference by counting fundamental string operations, like insertion, deletion, and substitution. Therefore the distances are obtained as metric for inner-class and inter-class, which is suitable for the k-means algorithm to cluster raw logs into groups. In the third step, in each cluster, raw log keys are examined iteratively to collect the information of the private part, not or almost not sharing with other individuals, and the common part, sharing with other keys. The information includes the position, count and belonging, by which pre-defined thresholds are used to split the cluster into several groups. Finally, inside each group, empirical rules form the eventual format followed by another edit distance to determine the main body of the entire group.

Makanju et al. propose a log invariant message iterative partitioning algorithm in [26, 28], called IPLoM (Iterative Partitioning Log Mining). The IPLoM removes Apriori algorithm to achieve computational efficiency by restricting hyper-parameters at minimal scale to stabilize the performance across multiple types of log sets, and ignores the system prior knowledge since accessing the source code into commercial software is always impossible. In detail, the algorithm consists of four main steps: *Partitioning by template length*, *Partitioning by a particular position*, *Partitioning by term mapping*, and *Abstracting the template*. Firstly, a similar assumption has been made, which is one underlying template always produces equal log messages with variables. By this assumption, the entire data will be scanned once to obtain candidate bins that temporarily hold raw logs. Inside one single bin, each position will be examined across all the logs and find out the number of unique tokens for each position. The intuitive is that the column with the least unique token is at least one of the constant entry in terms of its underlying log type, as variables will vary from a broad perspective resulting in massive amount unique values. Thirdly, the bijective mapping constructs the foundation of discovering a strong relationship between co-occurrence stable constants. The bijections come from the second and the third most frequent (most counts) unique tokens within a candidate bin. It is because at least one column remains the same thanks to the position-based partitioning. The bijection is the core operation of IPLoM taking the heuristics that stable mapping highlights the branches and the counts of mappings will be greater than 1. When the bijections are discovered, the logs with such bijections are split into corresponding candidate branch bins for the last extraction step. Lastly, to achieve abstraction that constants are kept and variables are substituted by wild cards $*$.

Although IPLoM outperforms other algorithms, some serious issues appear during partitioning. For instance, when using the mapping, logs that variable dominates the format type may cause so-called *M-M* relation. This type of relations will confuse the algorithm with multiple interpretable and legal candidates. The issue remains unsolved since the authors put it in the future work.

2.1.2   Statistics-based Network Fault Diagnosis

Statistics-based analysis is a common and traditional choice of network fault diagnosis to discover characteristics of system operation. For general network fault diagnosis, processing key performance indicators is also an informative and effective approach, for instance, [45–47], while this section reviews the statistics-based works applied to detect and analyze the root causes of infrastructure and distributed-style cloud computing systems. The core of log-based analysis is to represent the key features of discrete logs and transfer the features to the corresponding system behaviors, which can be regular operation or abnormal symptoms.

In addition to network low-level system, the recent distributed cloud computing mechanism has specific fault analysis requirements, since cloud computing exposes distinct interface and management plane. To provide reliable services and maintain robust performance, fault tolerance in cloud is of the essence and an imperative issue [48–51], which guarantees system sustainable operation to users even with occurrence of faults. In general, fault tolerance involves in two types of techniques: reactive approaches, including *checkpoint, job migration, Replication* and proactive approaches, including *self-healing, preemptive, system rejuvenation*. Note that fault tolerance is highly closely related to system-level decision and action in terms of automation or administrator-authorization. However, the main focus here is highly relevant to fault prediction, discovery, identification and localization, therefore fault tolerance is out of the research scope.

Beyond the academic perspective of log analysis, open-source and commercial processing pipelines and tools, such as logstash [52] and splunk [53], are developed to accommodate massive data and digest in either streaming or off-line scene. Processing pipelines can be built linking a series of compatible platforms [54] to become core analysis modules in a production-ready work-frame. These tools will firstly walk through the input data to recognize the global structure via matching off-the-shelf formats. Then the key characteristics are listed and illustrated visually via expert rules for system administrators to stimulate the conventional analysis process. Guided by the statistical properties across a particular time duration, analysts may reveal crucial operation status and dig out hidden time series-like anomalies.

Event Correlation Based Methods

As clarified above that logs are always interpreted as serialized system events or behaviors in terms of time, one widely accepted view is that the context events are highly temporal correlated and the correlation evidently entails strong systematic integrity, even causality for fault root localization [55, 56]. Some related research [57–59] have been done to utilize the statistical correlation to deduce black box-style operation status. A structured and thorough introduction and research direction analysis for event correlation is presented in [55].

In [57], it presents that influences which are defined by interactions between system modules can represent normal operation logic and behaviors through time-correlated events to unveil anomaly and misbehaviors. A Structure-of-Influence Graph (SIG) is constructed to make edges hold correlations and strengths between system components which were assumed to be black boxes. It proposes two models based on log message timing and log message content, respectively. One implicit assumption is that the log timing gaps can be quantified as anomaly signal and conform to a stable distribution. Recording the history distribution and computing the most recent timing distribution enable the calculation of Kullback-Leibler divergence [60] to be entries of signal matrices, which in turn are converted into a correlation matrix and a delay matrix. With the two matrices, the SIG is constructed and fed into the downstream system-dependent analyzers. It also provides two system analysis cases checking an autonomous vehicle operation [61] and a complex system of the Thunderbird supercomputer [25]

In [58], the authors put forwards a unified time-series detection framework for runtime change points identification. The change point, also called outlier, is defined as one or segment points outside the statistical regularity of histories, by which the margin deviated from the regularity is measured. Although the whole model targets at sequential data, the collection is network access time series coming from commonly used access logs. In fact, this method is very similar to the network access behavior frequency processing. Naturally, the model is named as *ChangeFinder* and is divided into two stages, fitting the time-series and identifying the significant changes. In the first stage, following a well-defined problem setting, an abstract scoring loss calculation is formulated with a probability density function, which is subsequently exemplified by an auto regression (AR) model [62] and a variant of maximum likelihood named as Sequential Discounting AR learning algorithm (SDAR). In the following detection stage, change point detection, a measure called *T-average score* within T time interval, is defined and two moving average processes are adopted to synthesize the first stage into the *T-average score*, which increases model robust in the meanwhile.

Yamanishi et al. [59] proposes a hidden markov model (HMM) [63] based dynamic event correlation discovery method for well formated syslog [64] data to output an anomaly degree.

The anomaly degree is compared against a dynamically flexible threshold to determine whether the warning should be flagged. To be more detailed, they firstly divided the syslog abstract event into several independently distributed sessions and fit the sessions in HMM mixture as a generative model. Secondly, a variant of *online discounting mixtures learning* algorithm, which is a type of *Expectation-Maximization*(EM) [65, 66], is employed to optimize HMM mixture parameters. To select the number of components of mixtures, a dynamic model selection(DMS) [67] is applied to fit in sequential and batched data conditions. Finally, the score formulation of a syslog event is given on top of its corresponding session probability distribution and the flexible threshold is implemented by an online style histogram of the recent score distribution. Though a time-aware threshold is in effect, a set of hyper-parameters are supposed to be set manually.

In [68], authors propose an analytical workflow, named *FDiag*, to cope with error diagnosis issues including log message template extraction, events correlation and operation sequence recognition. In message template extraction(MTE), the mining approach applies expert knowledge to separating *constants* and *variables* based on manual observation and administrators and implement in six steps. In the statistical event correlator, it lays the foundation of domain knowledge groups and pair-wise association heat-map to transfer event occurrence frequency matrix into Pearson correlation coefficient [69] matrix. In the third stage, the *Episode Constructor* extracts log events in one domain knowledge and makes the log events within a time window grouped into one *episode*, namely an operation trace, which eventually helps identify key events and diagnose the root cause of failures. The tool work admittedly effectively under some certain circumstances, however, system-dependent log contents observation prevents from extending to wider applications and generalizing to broader utilization.

Statistical Property Based Methods

Differing from mining and extracting the implicit event correlations, log events occurrence and co-occurrence statistical properties offer the possibility that discrete events can be turned into time based numerical features. The processing paradigm avoids unstable sequential corruption but keep the local real-valued features smoothly by conditioning the investigated data on a limited time interval. Some work involves in identifying real world events [70], nevertheless faults and anomalies are widely accepted as technical hazardous events taking place in network equipments. The review focuses mainly on issues with respect to computer networking.

Lim et al. [71] analyze the problem of detecting commercial telephony system failures in quantity and introduce frequency-related methods to unveil numerical trend from log events.

They suppose that empirical human knowledge that detects the system crash cause can be modeled numerically from log statistical characteristics to generalize to wider occasions. To implement it, the unstructured log messages are reduced into patterns based on modified Levenshtein distance, by which the original messages are substituted by the corresponding patterns afterwards. With the given event segments labeled as system failures, the particular signatures of interest is supposed to be extracted. At beginning, the frequent item set is mined based on event co-occurrence. Afterwards, overall message and individual message frequency are investigated to highlight unexpected count mutants and individual event-wise frequency trend. The obvious changes can be viewed as failure numerical signatures, which are taken as input the following application dependent clustering algorithm to identify failure trends.

In [72], the authors suppose that a sequence of log messages should implicitly hold a temporal dependency, which lays the foundation of time characteristics. In order to extract log patterns, named as categorization, the authors introduce modified Naive Bayes algorithm and Hidden Markov Model considering time stamps. Another claim they hold is that the abstract log events tend to unfold temporal information in terms of event causality. Also, they take the system parallelized operation into consideration as interarrival distributions. To tackle this problem, the occurrence order is integrated into conditional probability distributions, which are estimated by arrival time stamp and waiting durations. The significant relationships are finally tested and separated by Chi-squared test [73], evaluating incoming events whether appear within time window, which determines the relationships in statistics.

The above traditional scenario is to detect and localize faults in the scope of network elements and equipments predominantly based on temporal features, whereas significant spatial information, i.e., multi-layer, geographical location, and etc., is not fulled exploited [27]. In [27], the authors point out that the complex multiple-layer network architectures may corrupt the message correlations and hide vital information over inter-crossed log records, which should be taken serious consideration. Enhanced by the proposed statistical template extraction (STE) and the definition of template group and network event, the work takes approximate non-negative tensor factorization (NTF) approach [74, 75] and extends to log tensor factorization (LTF) to extract template groups and model event relationships. The main contribution of the work is mathematically formulating the log tensor factorization update through a special function, which stimulates the decomposition. In the end, three supportive and promising cases are presented with insights from the proposed LTF.

Admittedly, a proposed algorithm gives a clear clue and direction to settle a system fault problem for most of work, nonetheless a systematic tool with fully parsing, analysis and output functionality attracts more attention to pragmatist. In [76], authors contributes to an integrated error analysis system, named *SherLog*, including log type parsing, targeted system execution path inference, and execution value inference. In log parsing module, the approach assumes source codes are available and logging position in source codes are clarified by developers as well as retrievable logging severity. Promoted by abstract syntax tree (AST) [77] and extended regular expression, the parser supports basic and complex logging blocks. As for path inference, the approach employs Boolean satisfiability problem(known as propositional satisfiability problem, or SAT) solver [78] to discover and reconstruct full and partial execution path, called *Must-Paths* and *May-Paths*, respectively. The previous two steps are consistent with common fault diagnosis approaches, whereas *SherLog* adds a value inference stage as an extra analysis module to emphasize the importance of variables associated in logs across execution path. As the variable entries characterize the execution sequence and operation status, value inference is able to provide numerical analysis along with symbolic path execution inference. Their evaluation over failures like Apache, GNU core-utils, shows the effectiveness, but unfortunately the tool only works under the assumption that the source codes are retrievable and domain knowledge applies to link the value trend to fault propagation. A more scalable scheme is more preferable in practical applications.

2.1.3   Finite State Machine-based Network Fault Diagnosis

Event correlation-based and Statistics-based approaches basically focus on the log data itself involving in endeavor to grasp the abstract and discrete hidden attributes of logs. On the other hand, the interaction relationships between events and associated hidden system states are not merged into analysis schemes, though vital information may be conveyed by the interactions. Recently, finite state machine for system execution derivation by digesting text-based logs has drawn much attention and some effective algorithms have been employed [79–84]. In these works, [79] generates control-flow and data-flow execution traces to fit in finite state machine; [80] and [82] make efforts to reveal operational processes in the sense of information system by building Petri nets [85], which can mathematically represent system work trajectories or transition paths; [81], [83], and [84] apply event traces coarsening and refinement leveraging model checking techniques [86] to produce event occurrence graphs.

In detail, authors in [79] face the challenge of analysis of Hadoop distributed computing platform [87], which contains inter-arrival recorded events, developing a tool called **SALSA**. From the logs, the tool assumes the existence of time stamps, host names and tasks. Following the dissecting the of its log4j module, **SALSA** divisively extracts work-flow from Jobtracker, NameNode, TaskTracker and DataNode and discovers control-flow and data-flow, respectively, by identifying tokens of interests. Besides the description of the tool, the authors also provide two case studies of improving task allocation visualization and stimulating failure diagnosis heavily dependent on Hadoop working mechanism.

Authors in [80] focus on processing mining via discovering Petri nets [85] from sequential event data. The necessity of processing mining lies on issues of diagnosing historical processing and gaining insights to improve system operation. The Petri nets describe the processing in a sense of state transition with condition and activation action, which is suitable for collecting information and identify the key points of sequential logs. Petri nets also assist to cope with parallel and concurrent sequences that are intersected by each other even with noisy log data and incomplete sequence traces. Authors introduce a method called "α-algorithm" [88] and dedicate to applying its fundamental idea to mitigate the affect of noisy and incomplete sequential elements and concurrent processing. From a practical perspective, the Petri nets based invariants and implementations have been integrated in an open-sourced processing tool, called ProM [89], for the convenience of academic and industrial research.

The work in [81] mainly proposes a synthesized analysis tool, named "*Synoptic*" for inferring a system model to digest graph-like sequential behaviors, which is followed by [83], and [84] to deliberately improve and showcase the utility of it. Unlike the concurrent mixed task logs, the hypothesis of logged events is that a trace identifier is strictly tagged with log records that are bounded in one task. The trace identifier helps avoid tangled processes and discover the boundary of a task. With the explicit time stamps and abstract log types parsed by regular expressions, trace graphs are initially constructed in terms of the order in sequences and assign directed relations based on the log co-occurrence summary. An initial trace graph is inaccurate and seemingly chaotic. As such, after a trace graph initialization, two stages, refinement and coarsening, are deeply involved to finalize it in terms of competition. To be more specific, refinement attempts to separate oversimple graphs that shield fine-grained executions, in the meanwhile, coarsening attempts to drag the refinement back from unnecessary division to avoid extreme separation. The refinement stage employs the counterexample guided abstraction refinement (CEGAR) approach [90] to decide partitioning and the coarsening stage makes the use of the kTail-equivalence [91] to merge abundant branches as one united branch. The two stages present a behavior in terms of competition while it fails to achieve the global optimum without iterations, and this type of graph construction is a NP-hard problem [90]. More efficient algorithms are expected to obtain in the future work.

2.1.4 Deep Learning-based Network Anomaly and Fault Diagnosis

Deep Learning have prevailed in automatic, cognitive and scalable tasks during the recent decades thanks to the tremendous generalization and fitting ability [92]. One of the key reasons is the enormous prepared data facilitate the training processing in supervised fashion in applications like image processing [93], Natural Language Processing [94] and etc. With appropriate information and data, the data-driven approach apparently offers bonus for versatile tasks and applications. Specifically, networking environment is inclined to produce vast amounts of various log data, which definitely raises the difficulty of ingesting information but brings about more chances for Deep Learning based insightful digestion [2]. Furthermore in general anomaly detection research, Deep Learning still plays a significant role of engaging novel schemes and models even without manual labels for novelty identification [95]. Recent notable efforts are shown in Table 2.3, which commonly regards the log data as sequences with timely property and learnable in terms of Recurrent Neural Networks.

Table 2.3 Recent Efforts Based on Deep Learning for Network Anomaly and Fault Analysis

Research Work	Data Type	Formatting	Style	Model Block
[96]	Raw Text Log	Tokenization	Sequential	LSTM
[97]	Log Template	Template Extraction	Sequential	LSTM
[98]	Log Template	Template Extraction	Sequential	LSTM
[99]	Abstract Event	Not Applied	Sequential	LSTM
[100]	Log Template	Template Extraction	Sequential	LSTM

The work in [96] introduces a sequential probability learning based on the language modeling in Natural Language Processing for discrete token prediction. The high-level theory utilizes the Long Short Term Memory (LSTM) base as its model building block to construct a tiered framework that takes as input the tokenized data and wraps up the context. The input tokens come from the raw log data tokenization and are filtered by a frequency threshold. A word embedding [101] alike lookup table is adopted in order to properly fit the data into a numerical learning model. Apparently, the analysis grain stays on the frequent token-level instead of accounting for event-level logs. The attention mechanism [102] [103] is taken effect to capture the context. Normally, it puts the Softmax function as the probability approximation in the last step.

Authors in [97] name their framework of Deep Learning for System Health after *"Desh"* for short, clearly indicating the fundamentals that underlie the system health analysis. Unlike general anomaly and fault detection, the work focuses on predicting node failures over a large-scale high performance computing (HPC) system via system-level executions. The *Desh* framework consists of three stages, two training processes, failure chain learning and lead time failures prediction, and one test stage to validate its prediction model. Similarly, the *Desh* framework also takes as input frequent constant phrases that are embedded as vector representations. Moreover, the adopted sequential model takes the time gap between phrases into consideration to perceive the lead time rather than appearance of failures. The language model idea is similar to other research while the main difference is the work in *Desh* attempts to dive into exact lead time approximation.

In [98], *DeepLog* is proposed to fit a long term short memory (LSTM) model in natural language-like sequential log data. The framework endeavors to model hidden transactional patterns over abstract events that are transfered from raw messages to templates. It firstly considers unstructured log format parsing into template shape for noise elements reduction by *Spell* in [32]. Based on the OpenStack cloud computing platform [104], *DeepLog* further identifies and retrieve key values, such as task IDs and elapsed time, for its particular input parameter vector. As for the architecture, two stages, training and detection, constitute the core functionality. In training, the sequential parsed log templates associated with their parameter vectors are fed into a LSTM-based model. In detection, two steps binded with two modules are consecutively carried out to predict the forthcoming logs and further parameter vectors. The log prediction applies to execution path anomaly detection through sequential LSTM model as well as the parameter vectors that relate to the parameter vector and performance anomaly detection. In particular, *DeepLog* checks the parameter vectors with its original assigned log keys range, which is successfully transformed into multi-variable time-series detection process. The logs are marked as normal if and only if both tests are passed, and the anomalous information will be display to system administrators for further diagnosis.

Another relevant research is [100] based on recurrent neural learning from the perspective of Deep Learning, which consistently model sequential events as language prediction. The system failure prediction takes abstract events into account in terms of console logs that are the same as operation and execution logs. To recognize the patterns, namely template extraction, it adopts a hierarchical clustering algorithm named OPTICS [105] by widening observed data points towards adjacent data to retrieve a dense phrase. The *"dense"* here is restricted by a preset threshold. The patterns are subsequently used to omit variables from raw logs. Without soft representation learning, this work immediately employs the term frequency–inverse document frequency (TF-IDF) algorithm [106] to obtain the vectorized features that are pushed into the following LSTM model. Undoubtedly, the LSTM as an effective sequential modeling tool is prevalent over timely ordered log data analysis.

In contrast to systematic operation logs, authors in [99] propose *Tiresias* to focus on access security log on web service based platform targeting at adversaries triggered by attacks. They emphasize the contribution on exact future actions prediction rather than showing binary outcomes. Basically, the *Tiresias* leverages the LSTM recurrent blocks to receive sequential security events as language model alike framework, which is formulated to cope with variable length input. Different from event parsing preprocessing, *Tiresias* aims at well-defined access log events, such as HTTP and Apache server status, strongly associated with cyber-attacks. The further evaluation and case study shows the availability of *Tiresias* and its high precision.

2.2 Traffic Engineering for Network Management

Traffic Engineering (TE) is crucial for network management and the utility and performance of networks, for example Quality-of-Service (QoS), in the era of big data [7, 8]. It has been a hot-spot in recent research trend [7–11]. Technically, Traffic Engineering involves in multiple disciplines [107, 108, 7, 8], including network adaptive routing, traffic profiling, traffic classification, resource scheduling, load balancing, and etc., towards networking global utility optimization as its ultimate task. Each relevant area has a strong impact on network usage conditions and efficient, while in this thesis, the topic is dedicated to network data flexible and agile forwarding, routing and planning. Traffic Engineering has a strong and obvious binding with properly scheduling data forwarding and streaming involving in network performance and user experience improvement. In addition, software define network (SDN) is also highlighted as the data delivery platform of interests, since the SDN [109] impresses researchers and practitioners enormously with resilient programmability and effectiveness.

Though TE facilitates network control and management [7, 8], its challenges still remain and negatively affect network performance, for example, dynamic load balance using fine-grained control. Massively generated digit data in Big Data era bring about challenges, e.g. dealing with unformatted data and opportunities as well, e.g. implying abundant knowledge and information [110]. The implied knowledge may be the key for efficient traffic analysis and engineering. Also, the separated data plane and control plane enable control plane to have access global information and high level awareness of hidden state, making it suitable to merge data-driven model into centralized controller as an intelligence decision-maker [9].

Therefore, in section 2.2.1, efforts based on traditional models are reviewed and the novel Deep Learning inspired progresses are reviewed as following in section 2.2.2.

2.2.1 Classic Traffic Engineering for Network Management

As is manifest that the Traffic Engineering (TE) imposes crucial impact on network performance, it intrigues researchers to overcome serious in both stale network structure and novel programmable paradigm. In early network development and usage, Asynchronous Transfer Mode (ATM) and later Multi-protocol Label Switching (MPLS) emerge with Internet Protocol (IP) and the corresponding IP-routing technologies [111, 112], before the SDN underlies the fundamental functionality. A heuristic and preliminary adjustment is unsurprisingly flexible for simple and idle links if the requirement keeps low, however the robustness reduces dramatically when network flows persistently grow [111, 112]. Researchers have endeavored to carry out some notable ideas to relieve the pressures caused by network traffic congestions.

In early days, authors in [111] claim that the Open Shortest Path First algorithm (OSPF) present and Intermediate System-Intermediate System (IS-IS) give an acceptable and efficient intuition for on-demand IP traffic delivery in general IP network. The above two methods tend to search an optimal path for a transferring request in a network topology with stable link weights. The adjustable and dynamic link weights configuration is available to maintain high quality of service. For instance, the work in [113] as well as [114] attempts to overcome the issue raised by the OSPF and IS-IS with a static link weights setting, which helps traffic routing scheme to make the most use of bandwidth capacity and reduce packet loss. In addition to next-hop routing fashion based on the OSPF, another effective approach is to split a given traffic flow into several sub-flows and distribute into multiple links [115, 116], each of which will the equal resource consumption. It can be sometimes called as Equal-Cost-MultiPath, *"ECMP"* [116]. Opposed to immediate shortest path and IS-IS routing mechanism, the multiple path distribution helps with adaptive traffic load balance, switch end controlling, flexible quality guarantee and etc., without extra overhead and protocol modification. However, flow distribution to multiple paths brings about packet disordering issues and always require existing multiple shortest paths as decision region. An intuitive method is to close the gap between the path prediction and distribution without changing underlying routing protocol, which is the core effort of work in [117]. It actively selects a fraction of all shortest paths and distributes some flows with particular prefix accordingly, ultimately approximating the optimal performance.

The advent of the SDN architecture [118, 119] as the novel programmable network paradigm facilitates networking evolution for services of higher quality as well as challenges for traffic engineering [8, 112], for instance dynamic load-balance for both data and control plane. From a broader view of Traffic Engineering, authors in [7] put forward a conceptual framework seeking to divide the process as two parts, traffic measurement and traffic management, which is ambitiously expected to integrate existing advances into uniform object. To be detailed in concrete practices, authors in [120] solely focus on parts of forwarding elements that make up of the data plane and support its functionality, meanwhile the rest of network maintains the standard routing mechanism. The part of interest is portrayed and formulated as a problem minimizing packet delay and loss surrogated by link utilization optimization, which is eventually tackled by a Fully Polynomial Time Approximation Scheme (FPTAS). A similar idea is leveraged and realized by Segment Routing (SR) [121], which allows hosts to transmits data via a handful marked segments instead of trivial fine-grained hops. The SR technique is well compatible with the SDN control and data plane [122] simplifying node-by-node arrangement as coarse-grained forwarding, which consequently influences several following works [123–125].

2.2.2 Deep Learning-based Traffic Engineering

Machine Learning and the further progresses of Deep Learning regulate the hidden structural information and in turn exploit the patterns to consolidate the understanding of objects, which is able to seamlessly engage in complex networking with huge data pool [126–129, 6, 130, 108, 9]. In this section, Deep Learning is the main target of investigation for its remarkable achievements in many domains[131, 93, 94, 92, 132]. Normally, one latent hypothesis for Deep Learning related techniques is the magnitude of data supports to discover the distribution that the data conform to. Even though the complexity may confuse the learning model, the expressive techniques in Deep Learning can elastically generalize to broader range. As for networking in terms of traffic engineering, loads of real time streams are flowing across the communication apparatuses and ubiquitous network equipments persistently generate operation-related information. Large size and heterogeneous data inevitably cause difficulty in efficient analysis and computation, meanwhile the Deep Learning model benefits from abundant data to mine valuable knowledge. Recently, numerous efforts for general networking mechanism and the SDN have been made by researchers and practitioners in both academia and industry. Besides general large-scale carrier network, the Deep Learning paradigm also makes for wireless and 5G network a shift towards intelligent and automatic management [133, 134, 11]. A brief summary for most recent and noteworthy research contributions are listed in Table 2.4.

Traffic Routing And Forwarding Strategy

For improvement of routing strategy, works in [135, 136, 139, 145, 138, 146] all attempt to exploit abundant information to accomplish optimal traffic forwarding decision.

Specifically, it proposes a Deep Belief Net (DBN)-based architecture in [135] for flexible routing table construction oriented at Software Defined Router (SDR) that can be accelerated by Graphic Processor Unit (GPU). The model predicts the next routing sequential nodes taking traffic patterns in edge routers as input through data collected with pairs of traffic patterns and routing paths. In contrast to traditional routers, the SDR is devised to dynamically embed strategies and provide programmability regardless of the limitations of hardwares.

Table 2.4 Recent Efforts Based on Deep Learning for Traffic Engineering

Research Work	Method	Objective Network	Application	Data
[135]	DBNs	Software Define Router	Routing Decision	Traffic Patterns
[136]	CNN-DL	Wireless SDN	Routing Decision	Topology & Traffic Attributes
[137]	CNN-DL	Wireless Network	Partially Overlapping Channel Assignment	Traffic Patterns
[138]	CNN-DRL	SDN	Routing Decision	Network Graph Information
[139]	CNN-DL	Wireless Network	Routing Decision	Time Interval Tensor
[10]	DRL	SDN	Multiple Paths Decision	Traffic Throughput & Delay
[140]	DRL	SDN	Multiple Paths Decision	Flow Statistics
[11]	DRL	Cellular Network	Multiple Paths Decision	Measurement & Traffic Patterns
[141]	DRL	Wireless Network	Cache Enable Opportunistic Interference	Requested Content Status
[142]	DRL	SDN	Multimedia Traffic Control	Traffic Measures
[143]	DRL	Edge Computing	Off-loading	Task Measures
[144]	DRL	Named Data Networking	Congestion Control	Traffic Measures
[145]	Graph CNN-DL	SDN	Routing strategy	Network Measures
[146]	RNN	SDN	Routing strategy	Network Measures
[147]	DRL	SDN	Timeout Mechanism	Traffic Measures
[148]	Graph NN-DL	Wireless Network	Channel Schedule	Geographic Location Information

The traffic patterns are defined as inbound packets volumes within several time intervals. The model is designed in Deep Belief Net structure in supervised training fashion, where two extra layers of Restricted Boltzmann Machine are stack for data reconstruction training.

In [136], authors give an overview of SDN integrated with wireless network merging as Software Defined Wireless Networks (SDWN) and point out the drawbacks of the conventional shortest path routing. Therefore they propose to employ Convolutional Neural Networks (CNN) as a feature learner and extractor of input traffic patterns. The proposed model takes input as traffic patterns in terms of source-destination paired matrix instead of numerical vectors. Furthermore, the matrix is expanded as sliced tensors with respect to different metric types, which fits better in the CNN model than the fully connected layers. With the benefit of SDN structure, the control plane makes computational decisions and deploys into switches in data plane.

Tang et al. [139] consider more general wireless network backbone scenario for intelligent and real time traffic control scheme to avoid congested traffics. Their objective metrics are average packet delay and packet loss, which are heavily influenced by the routing decisions. The issue of routing is formulated as the combinatorial optimization as well as conventional shortest path construction while the solution should be more dynamic and adjustable for novel situations. Then a real-time CNN-based model is proposed to receive multi-dimensional traffic patterns to predict a next forwarding hop. The traffic patterns are also defined by the interval packet generation ration in terms of router pairs. A traffic patterns matrix is viewed as a status slice with respect to various measurements to form a 3-order tensor or a 3-D traffic matrix. The tensor is input into a CNN feature extractor and output the final prediction probability over all the available routers, based on which the most likely one is deemed as the chosen router.

The above several research works focus on traffic patterns implication by a standard CNN block, however the nature and property of network topological information have been ignored. The potential problem of lacking of structural information is lacking of correct direction and convergence. Authors in [145] leverage graph-related processing to perceive the topological and spatial correlations in a network. Inspired by graph learning methods, a graph-aware deep learning framework is proposed for intelligent routing solution in supervised learning fashion. The deep learning framework is also enhanced by the CNN block to learning structural features. To expressive represent a network topology, a set of well-defined adjacency and measures matrices, including link attributes and transmission statistics, are constructed to capture the local structure. The core idea is to find neighbors of each vertex in consistent way in case disordered graph traverse and the number of neighbors is fixed set as k. The captured neighbors are formed as the neighbor-of-interest matrices. These matrices are paralleled applied with standard CNN kernels and subsequently with feed forward output layer for node prediction.

Apart from the conventional networking, researchers in [138] investigate the network management scenario that the algorithms and applications are virtualized in accelerating infrastructures with computing resource, for example Heterogeneous Computing Platform. Researchers attempt to deploy Deep Reinforcement learning into the Heterogeneous Computing Platform, making the strategy node into the controller. As for reinforcement learning, the routing strategy learning process is formulated as Markov Decision Process (MDP) and value iteration based Q-learning is adopted as decision-making. With the assistant of CNN as the feature learning block, the model takes the network structure information and traffic source-destination pair information as input to estimate the total value that a series taken-actions can return. Additionally, the implementation in controller and router is different to separate training and routing application.

Zuo et al. [146] circumvent the usage of CNN model to grasp the network implication. Instead, they dedicates to learning the implications of the traffic sequence itself through Recurrent Neural Networks (RNN) based model. The hypothesis is that several constrains are likely to be applied to routing such as load balancing and firewall. The authors consider the routing path constrains on accessing particular node as a predictable path planning problem. To automatically plan the constrained path, historical experiences are utilized as training input. Inspired by the sequence-to-sequence technique in language machine translation, the sequence-to-sequence model is employed as path transformation between the transferring source-destination pair and forwarding path. The sequential model building block is a LSTM model, in the meanwhile, the transformation is improved with Attention mechanism and beam search to obtain global optimums. The evaluation shows the deep learning model is able to mine the hidden sequential patterns in traffic path experience and serve as a decision-maker for stable path planning.

Traffic Distribution In Multiple Paths

Routing strategy related works endeavor to plan a concrete traffic deploying path and implement the regulations into programmable switches. The method is straightforward and assigns an optimal or approximately optimal option to a communication request. In this regard, a communication session is comprised of and binded with the particular path. The complexity of computation is relatively high due to the incremental communication sessions and the growing number of forthcoming requests. Apart from picking switches node-by-node, assume that there would have several available path options that could be obtained by the OSPF algorithm, the problem can be transformed to jointly distributing traffic flows in all options. An extreme case is to reduce into a traditional routing strategy, where a flow is fully deployed solely in one of the shortest alternatives. As normal usage, traffic flows are proportionally and adaptively split into all or some of the paths for optimized performance defined as the network utility.

The work in [10], named Deep Reinforcement Learning Traffic Engineer (DRL-TE), and its successor [140], named Deep Reinforcement Learning for Congestion Control (DRL-CC), share the fundamental solution cores that traffic split ratio determination can be modeled as a Markov Decision Process. The action-taken is the deploying proportion over given communication tunnels so that the action space is inherently continuous and countless rather than discrete and limited. To target at the network utility maximization (NUM) in the Multi-Path TCP (MPTCP) applications, both of them carefully consider the variants of Deep Deterministic Policy Gradient (DDPG) [149] for adjusting to continuous actions applications. Nonetheless, the observed states are very different. In [10], the states are regarded as a space of session throughput and delay, where the state representation is formed as a 2-tuple element vector. In [140], the states warp up the states of each flow including sending rate, throughput, statistics of Round Trip Time (RTT), and congestion widow size. The numerical representation learning methods have also adopted to implement interpretable computation, fully connected neurons in [10] and LSTM in [140], respectively. The reward settings are particularly designed for either effort. For the former work, α-fairness [150] is denoted as the network utility and the reward. For the latter, the authors propose a close-loop framework which is not limited in a specific reward function and accept the average goodput statistics [151] in empirical evaluation.

In addition to networking infrastructures, the authors in [11] consider the High Volume Flexible Time (HVFT) applications in the field of Internet of Things (IoT) via wireless cellular network architecture. The HVFT applications are triggered by various and trivial instances in IoT with vast amount of small and large flow requests. The requests can be tiny software updates, daily device reports, and timely measurements, etc., which do not require real time and stable communication, and are delay-tolerant. However, the HVFT traffics may consume a huge ratio of transmission bandwidth congesting real-time requests due to the lack of appropriate scheduling. Therefore, a Reinforcement Learning-base algorithm is proposed to optimize the networking scheduling scheme allowing the efficiency of HVFT as well as the quality of non-tolerant services. With the standard MDP framework, the state is defined as a combination of current network state and temporal information of histories. The current network state contains congestion metric, session number and cell efficiency. The temporal information is extracted from time-series-form network states by a conceptual extractor which can be realized by time-series data processors, i.e., the LSTM block. Then the reward function is inferred from desired traffic metrics and conventional performance loss. In contrast to prevalent model-free methods, a model-based state dynamics representation is formalized as transition mapping, which transfers a non-MDP issues into a standard MDP in another anger. The affected term is the congestion metric showing piecewise formulation in terms of the HVFT traffic scheduling proportion.

Other Traffic Engineering Problems

Authors in [137] attempt to face the problem of partially overlapping channels assignment (POCA) in the wireless SDN for the IoT scenario. The channels assignment issue rises due to heterogeneous networking infrastructure configurations and inappropriate association with busty and unstable links. The nature of dynamics heavily damages the working conditions and desired performance when conventional static algorithms are adopted. This work investigates several existing methods and concludes that the wireless channels allocation based the current traffic loads fails to cope with dramatically changing flows. In order to enable intelligent processing, a deep learning based traffic prediction method is utilized to learn the traffic temporal patterns and outline potential fluctuation. The empirical traffic pattern data are fed into a CNN-based learning model to output the possibility of all available channels. A closed-loop framework has been proposed with two phases, updating, and on-line and off-line training phases. The centralized controller design helps to keep the accuracy with global information collection.

In contrast to traffic analysis and applications, authors in [141] mention wireless channel and link utility optimization with two relevant technologies, caching and interference alignment (IA). Wireless proactive caching helps mitigate the link burden imposed by backhaul traffic loads and the IA reduces the affect of channel interference, both of which depend on the channel state information (CSI). Due to the unstableness of CSI in the context of ever-changing wireless environment, conventional techniques fail to capture the real patterns of CSI and have difficulty in accurate CSI prediction. As such, the authors formulate the cache-enabled opportunistic IA paradigm as a Markov Decision Process, and based on the formulation, a Deep Q-learning based method is employed to learn a policy for optimal IA user selection. The reinforcement learning module regards the channel coefficients and cache states as the joint states and determines which candidate user can be activated to allocate resources.

In [142], authors aim at the particular traffic engineering problems caused by multi-media traffic. For specific traffic management, for example, multi-media traffic, the metrics-sensitivity are required to take deep consideration. Multi-media applications now account for a large fraction of total flows residing in the network system and are highly sensitive to several metrics, e.g., delay, bandwidth, and packet loss, etc., which has drawn crucial attention to researcher. Same as other works, the SDN architecture underpins the centralized controlling scheme with the implementation of a Deep Reinforcement Learning decision-maker. The work in [142] considers the quality of experience (QoE) as the synthesized measurement for delay, throughput and other discrete metrics, and makes optimizing QoE as the total object. Five discrete metrics are mapped into one reward representation by a fully connected evaluation network as well as the state of flows for the actor-critic network structure. The actions in this work are different from others, consisting of two parts for exact control, the allocated path and feasible bandwidth not exceeding the maximal limit. Deep Deterministic Policy Gradient (DDPG) is subsequently taken as the advantageous update paradigm over standard Q-learning.

For emerging network model, the Named Data Networking (NDN) [152] in the information-centric networking (ICN) [153] plays a key role for the future content-based communication Internet architecture. The work in [144] devotes to meeting requirement of traffic management for the Named Data Networking, where the content is of special interest for the pull requests from users. Then a Deep Reinforcement Learning based Congestion Control Protocol (DRL-CCP) is proposed for tackling the complexity and dynamics in the NDN. Unlike the routing TCP requests, NDN focuses on content-sensitive information for users so that the resource allocation is to schedule flows in terms of requested content rather than forwarding prediction. Ten elemental variables are selected as the environment state and a content-based utility function is denoted as reward function to guide the policy to gain maximal total content utility. The action here is defined as the size of sending window of contents.

Deep Learning enhanced techniques are applied into other applications, for instance, [147] for rule timeout mechanism adjustment in SDN also based on Deep Q-learning, and [148] for channel scheduling in wireless network based on Graph neural networks to capture spatial information. It is manifest from these successful examples, the deep learning related paradigm fits well in the centralized SDN architecture and promotes the utility of networking through various applications. The integrity of deep learning and networking will make further progress in the future intelligent management and maintenance.

Chapter 3

Network Systematic Event Discovery and Anomaly Detection

3.1 Introduction

The goal of this chapter is to identify suspicious events based on available execution status, such as service execution logs and service query traces, and to raise necessary alerts to avoid catastrophic failures for a system. The idea is that using service execution logs can capture functional behaviors in a temporal manner and using query traces is able to capture systematic behaviors in a spatial manner, which will be introduced later. They sufficiently contain fine-grained and coarse-grained status. Combining them is supposed to enable expected detection conduction, and the experiment results well validate this hypothesis.

This chapter applies distributed dense representation of a complete transaction to learning regularity of each type of transactions and isolating execution outliers in such representational space. The traditional anomaly detections prefer statistical properties of logs, but rarely appreciate the practical role of generic events. One obvious difference between traditional systems and cloud-based distributed system is remote procedure calling [154] or RESTful API [155]. There is a chance that semantic log representation remains reasonable while service requests are pushed into an unexpected long queue raising timeout.

In this chapter, abstract events are firstly extracted to substitute parameterized text contents. Then mapping the discrete contents into real-valued vector space as mathematical explanation of transactions. Additionally, capturing query durations between subroutines to construct trace matrix as service calling representation helps aggregate multiple facets of transactions. Lastly, two representations are concatenated to feed into one-class classification to identify unexpected outliers.

3.2   An Overview of System Structure

We firstly introduce the proposed detection framework for the system with micro-services architectures, which focuses on two core aspects: individual service execution and services remote query. The former refers to whether a local single service can handle an incoming task properly within a reasonable time scale. The latter refers to whether the global lightly-coupled services as a whole can process a user request smoothly in an acceptable time. The local and global functionalities can be regarded as *two-tier behavior features* being encoded into mathematical and learnable representations in a distributed vector space.

In order to achieve the primary goal of runtime anomaly detection, the proposal builds two parallel representation learning procedures that can capture the above two core features. Fig. 3.1 illustrates the diagram of the proposal. The arrows are the data-flow as well as the proposal work-flow.

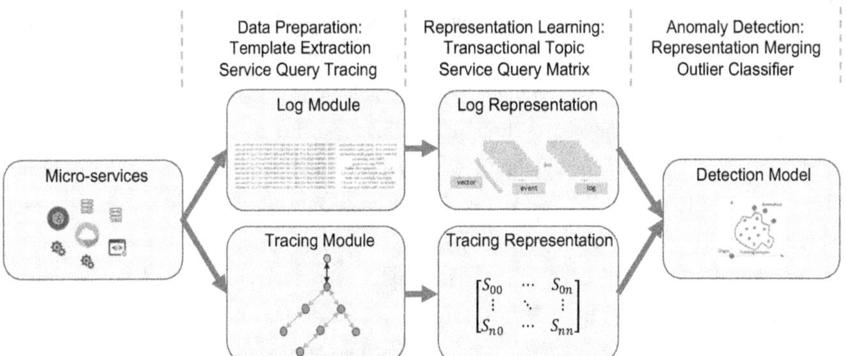

Fig. 3.1 The Proposed Framework for Runtime System Anomaly Detection in A Micro-services Architecture

In detail, it is divided into three stages: data preparation, representation learning, and anomaly detection. The first two stages analyze local and global behaviors. In data preparation, meta-execution logs are collected by the embedded logging module in the microservices architecture, and the hierarchical trace data sheets are collected by tracing probes. In addition, event templates are extracted from logs, and in turn chaotic logs shall be transferred into the template formation. In representation learning, the log template formation is mapped into distributed vectors to collectively infer a *"topic"* vector for a particular transaction. The tracing representation is extracted from the trace data sheet which is organized in hierarchy to expose request-response time. The representation is a matrix, each entry of which indicates a service duration queried from a front-end service to a certain back-end service. For the convenience of afterwards feature merging, the matrix is flattened along row as a sparse vector. In the last stage, two representation vectors are combined and merged as one vector containing local and global information. The joint features are then input into an outlier classifier to learn an implicit normal sample distribution, with which the classifier keeps the capacity of marking data out of the implicit distribution as anomalies. The experiment and evaluation platform is based on OpenStack cloud computing architecture [104], which implements each service component, e.g., nova-compute, neutron-networking, and keystone-authorization, by RESTful API based on the microservices architecture.

3.3 Event Template Extraction

In event template extraction, the aim is to distinguish and omit unstable variate entries to rewrite one single log in a compact and abstract manner. It is very clear that extracting templates involves in several distinct types of previous work from statistics to longest common subsequence, and from clustering to entry partitioning. Each of these algorithms is underpinned by different assumptions, like digits as variables, constants occupying the majority, logging source code and location is available and etc. Many proposals only apply to certain situations and have strict limitation. This thesis proposes partitioning-based log parsing methods to meet general requirements and keep high efficiency. In the thesis, terms like template, pattern and log type, are used interchangeably since they all indicate abstract representations of unstructured raw log messages.

As aforementioned, in general raw log message refers to the unstructured part written in natural language instead of fixed defined entities, like time stamp, host name, and severity. A template refers to a frequent item set with fixed position, explicit meaning and time invariant. A template of one or one groups of raw logs refers to the item set is entailed in these similar log messages excluding wild card $*$ that replaces infrequent variables.

Table 2.1 and Table 2.2 show the practical outcomes intuitively presenting the downward closure property [156], also known as Apriori property, by which unstructured and natural language-related log messages are compressed to compact text form. The compression can be seen as a surjective function from a raw log set to a template set formulated as:

Definition 3.3.1. Let $f_{ext} : R \rightarrow T$ be the extraction function that maps raw log set R into template set T, where $R = \{l_1, l_2, ..., l_N\}, N \in \mathbb{N}, T = \{t_1, t_2, ..., t_M\}, M \in \mathbb{N}, n \geqslant m, l_n$ denotes one raw log message, and t_m denotes one template.

To be specific, the raw log set R can be divided into $G = \{l_{\xi_1}, l_{\xi_2}, ..., l_{\xi_M}\}$ such that $l_{\xi_1} \cap l_{\xi_2} \cap ... \cap l_{\xi_M} = \varnothing$, and $l_{\xi_1} \cup l_{\xi_2} \cup ... \cup l_{\xi_M} = R$. For the i-th group, $l_{\xi_i} = \{l_1^i, l_2^i, ..., l_k^i\} \subseteq R$, where $1 \leq k \leq N$ and $l_{\xi_i} \subseteq R$, the corresponding template is obtained by $t_i = f_{ext}(l_\xi^i), t_i \in T, 1 \leq i \leq M$.

From the definition and subsequent properties, the cardinality of template set T is M equal to the cardinality of group set G. One raw log message can and only can be mapped into one template. Two extreme conditions can be clarified: 1.) $M = 1$ since all the messages entail the same template; 2.) $N = M$ since each message entail each unique template. A universal objective of the function is to minimize the cardinality of template set to cover wider raw messages but maximize the reserved information to express human readable events.

For minimizing the cardinality of template set, it attempts to discover the highly concise and succinct symbolic representations to generalize to sufficiently large groups of raw messages. In this manner, systematic interpretation would be concentrated on low dimensional space to avoid being overwhelmed by data flood. An example can be drawn from Table 2.1 and Table 2.2.

Raw logs:
l_1 = CE SYM 2, AT 0X0B85EA80, MASK 0X08
l_2 = CE SYM 21, AT 0X110035E0, MASK 0X80
l_3 = CE SYM 2, AT 0X0B85EA80, MASK 0X08
Ideal representation:
t = CE SYM * AT * MASK *

From the above example, the abbreviations and words are of interests instead of the specific numbering and digital physical address. Hence in the ideal representation, unstable marks are refined and the meaningful words are kept, and three abundant logs are converged into one sentence, $t = f_{ext}(l_i)$.

For maximizing the reserved information, the extraction function should disambiguate templates by divisive raw logs if the intrinsic events differ from among each other. If the diversity of template stays low, a direct result is to confuse analysis models and human administrators with substantial same event representations. In this manner, the extraction function should unfold abundant events by lowering the percentage of wild card $*$. Also from the above example, *"CE SYM * * * * *"* apparently can cover more types while losing discrimination capacity for administrator and the following diagnosis model, if the last four entries deliver other operations.

3.4   Partitioning-based Log Template Extraction

In [26, 28], the authors propose a successful log entry partitioning based method, called IPLoM to iteratively refine abstract candidates and use invariant entry pair mapping to obtain templates. As a matter of fact, the entire raw logs are seemingly irregular, chaotic and non intuitive. The partition and conquer [157] idea offers a graceful mechanism. The method proposed in this chapter is inspired by the IPLoM, since the partitioning follows the idea of fixed entry positions.

A drawback from [26, 28] is that the IPLoM assumes the message contain stable structures of words pairs. The assumed property fails to hold if developers tend to mark divisive executions with the same syntax and prefix. The same syntax will appear in the IPLoM partitioning candidates, entail pair mapping and eventually mislead the discriminator to unify variant templates. IPLoM is at the risk of masking key information with wild cards. The proposed partitioning-based extraction in the chapter discards the intuitive mapping finding and recursively partitions candidate sub-groups by the same mechanism as the first partitioning trial. As the algorithm here targets at the whole log data set, it is called the bulk-oriented recursive partitioning algorithm. Three steps in total are included and presented in the following.

3.4.1　Bulk Recursive Partitioning

First of all, it is broadly accepted that raw logs which entail the identical template would keep the same sentence length, namely entry count. Recall that the count relates to splitting a text sentence by given separators, i.e., space, tabs and any other given English punctuations. Thus one reasonable way to reduce entire raw log intersection chaos is to coarsely segment the equal length raw logs as several sub groups. The sub groups with equal length help identify and locate stable constants by columns alignment. Step one is the same as IPLoM.

After grouping raw logs with the identical sentence length (word count separated by space), in the second step, the first partitioning is based on the most stable entry position. The most stable entry position can be decided by the count of unique words occurring in that particular position. On top of the same sentence length, the group of messages can be aligned and fitted in a symbolic "matrix", of which each entry is a discrete word. This "matrix" is reduced into a vector with respect to column, by filling each place with the unique word count in the corresponding column. The column of the least one is chosen, where individual logs with the same entry word will be moved into one sub-group. At the moment, step two is also the same as IPLoM, nevertheless, the above operation is taken subsequently and recursively over the newly created sub-groups until a limit is reached.

That is, for one sub-group, one symbolic "matrix" is also temporally instantiated and compress into one vector. At this point, one difference is to ignore any column counting one to ensure the partitioning effect will not be taken repeatedly and unnecessarily over analyzed columns. A threshold of number of columns that count one is set to terminate the recursion process. The threshold controls how many seemingly constant words should remain to represent the event and how much information should be exposed to analyzers. The recursion process and threshold indicate the balance between minimizing cardinality of template set and maximizing the reserved information. The low threshold is inclined to extend one type as broadly as possible, meanwhile the high threshold tends to richen template diversity.

Once all the sub-groups become indivisible, the partitioning phase comes to the end and the final step results in generating template set or so-called template library, one template for each sub-group. At this point, the first one message would be examined along with the unique word counts vector, and words at any position corresponding to non-one, would be directly substituted by $*$, otherwise are kept. The template set storing all extracted templates is the ultimate outcome of the recursive processing.

Algorithm 1: Bulk-oriented Recursive Partitioning Algorithm

Data: Entire log message part, R
Parameter : Threshold, Thr
Result: A template library, lib_{part}
Initialize a set of candidate sets S_{entire};
for *message $l \in R$* **do**
    $l_{split} = split(l)$, via pre-defined symbols;
    length $= len(l_{split})$, length of the list l_{split};
    if *length not match any set in S_{entire}* **then**
        create a empty set $S_{\mathbf{length}}$ in S_{entire};
        append l in $S_{\mathbf{length}}$
    else
        append l in the matched $S_{\mathbf{length}}$
    end
end
Initialize a group of partitioned sets $Group_{part}$;
for *candidate set $S_{\mathbf{length}} \in S_{entire}$* **do**
    $Group_{part} = \text{RECUR\_PARTITION}(S_{\mathbf{length}}, Thr)$;
end
Initialize a library of templates;
for *one_set $\in Group_{part}$* **do**
    Replacing columns without count-1 unique terms with $*$;
    lib_{part} appends the processed content;
end
return lib_{part};

The partitioning detail is presented in **Algorithm 1**. In **Algorithm 1**, a parameter, Thr is required to determine remained information, which is ready for downstream tasks or semantic analysis. The function *Recursive Partitioning* takes as input a group of candidate sets and

---

Algorithm 2: Recursive Partitioning

Data: A set of logs
Parameter: *log_subset, INFO_threshold*
Result: A template set, *inner_set*
Function Recur_Partition(*log_subset,INFO_threshold*):

    split_set ← *log_subset* split by the column of the least unique terms;
    Initializing *inner_set* to hold partitioned set;
    for *one_block* ∈ *split_set* **do**
        if *Count 1 terms exceeds threshold* **then**
            append the block into *inner_set*;
            continue;
        else
            RECUR_PARTITION(one_block, INFO_threshold);
        end
    end
    Return *inner_set*;
End Function;

---

recursively output partitioned results. Afterwards, a template library, lib_{part} is returned and each entry of the library refers to one template.

3.4.2   Segmented Library Iteration

The bulk-oriented recursive partitioning algorithm will return satisfactory template library which is optimized against the original messages. However, one crucial disadvantage is the operation time consumption. Though there is information threshold controlling process depth, extreme examples include the messages that are chaotic and only small fragments of messages confirm to one template, which complicates and multiplies the recursion process into pieces. Inside the pieces, recursing until threshold has been reached can examine the single messages line by line repeatedly, which will grow rapidly with the message size. Another disadvantage is that bulk partitioning requires an off-line environment feeding the entire log dataset, which may compromise the log collection module and its efficiency.

Therefore, we propose a segmentation style log partitioning and an aggregation scheme to increase utility. The segmentation and aggregation extend the off-line scheme to not only on-line but also a parallel architecture, as the on-line scheme iterates streaming data to complete the template library, and the parallel architecture encourages local computing and low communication overhead.

The downward closure property [156] is introduced, also known as Apriori property, by which unstructured and natural language-related log messages can be compressed to compact text form. The downward closure property claims if a term set is frequent, then any subset should be at least as frequent as this term set. The property makes it possible that the frequent terms are obtained in segmentation, and the shared subsets are extracted in aggregation. In the segmentation step, **Algorithm 1** is only applied to a fraction of original logs, for example 1000 samples, which is determined by a split parameter. If in on-line manner, the fraction depends on the buffered streaming events, also pre-set by a buffer parameter. Apparently, the outputs are locally optimal, since no global information is considered. The intermediate template sets are stored as inputs to the aggregation step. Subsequently, the aggregation step takes the gathered intermediate templates as input to apply **Algorithm 1** again. At this point, the intermediate templates that are considered as "incomplete logs" entail the global information to approach more abstract forms. Details are described in **Algorithm 3**.

Algorithm 3: Segmentation and Aggregation

Data: Entire log message part, R
Parameter : Threshold, Thr;
              Log count in segments, $Seg\_interval$
Result: A template library, lib_{part}
Separating the entire log set sequentially with volume set by $Seg\_interval$;
$Seg\_list = \text{split}(R)$;
for $block \in Seg\_list$ **do**
    | Applying **Algorithm 1** to the block;
    | $temporal_lib = $ **Algorithm 1**$(block)$
end
Applying Aggregation to $temporal\_lib$;
$lib_{part} = Aggregation(temporal\_lib)$;
return lib_{part};

In addition to directly applying **Algorithm 1** in an on-line scheme, it is also reasonable to consider that the constant terms could exceed a fraction of variable terms in aggregation rather than adhering to a fixed information threshold. A case is that the count of constants should not be less than a percentage of the count of variables. The modification benefits relatively long logs from potential discovering the templates with majority of variables. It is obvious that in aggregation, it provides an interface of some adjustments to flexibly tackle extreme conditions, denoted as *Aggregation* in **Algorithm 3**. This modification referred to as *elastic aggregation*. The downward closure property guarantees log templates will gradually converge to its optimal abstraction. It is because within a local part of logs, variables, e.g., host names, are likely remain stable and are therefore inseparable. Nevertheless, on a longer timescale, the inseparable positions become chaotic and separable in terms of unique counts. The segmentation focuses on small fractions of data to relief computing pressure, meanwhile aggregation gathers intermediate results from segmentation to approximate optimal abstraction. The two steps manage to avoid large time consumption while gaining theoretical convergence.

3.5 Transaction-level Representation Learning

This section is to discuss the semantic representation of grouped logs, which are always entangled within a short period. The semantic learning collects execution information and will be the first half of the eventual transaction representation.

Though the preprocessing mainly involves in individual log record structures, the downstream tasks require deep analysis and comprehensive explanation in higher hierarchy. In other words, single individual log messages only record meta-execution, i.e., add and delete, send and receive, etc. The issues of meta-executions can express *error* or *critical* in log severity, while no evident signs will probably be expressed in case of system-level faults, for instance, the chaotic execution order causing service failure. The semantic analysis is to observe and discover hidden running patterns and make use of them to diagnose root causes.

A reasonable solution to high level events representation is to gather a group of logs sequentially occurring in a time-window and summarize its "*topic*" to a more compact and expressive format. The expressive formats shall compactly capture the corresponding systematic information and avoid effect of absolute message volume. In this manner, several fundamental factors should be taken into consideration. Firstly, logs shall be converted into template form to indicate events instead of unique individuals. The conversion depends on the outputs of the template extraction method and informative templates prevents identical events divergence. Secondly, the collected logs shall keep the original order since the execution sequence is one of the dominant factors which heavily influences decision. A widely accepted argument is that the execution order entails essential work-flow and its disorder and incompleteness possibly imply an abnormal task. Thirdly, the time-window shall be set properly and flexibly to ensure covering close related events and omitting long-standing disturbance issues, e.g., daemon procedures. Last but not least, the expressive "*topic*" shall be capable of keeping core content, compressing in a compact space and simplifying subsequent numerical computation.

The framework employs the previous template library, transaction request information and natural language analysis to address these factors. As for the first two points, issues are straightforward. All the raw messages are scanned line by line, each of which is aligned with one example in the template library. In practice, one way to reduce computation complexity is to only consider examples with the same length. Afterwards, all positions corresponding to asterisks would be masked to give way to matching other positions. Once conversion is finished, the whole data set becomes a sequence of meta-executions excluding unstable variables. In terms of the time window, a basic idea is using a pre-defined fixed scale to separate logs. However, the segments either may lose a significant part of logs or mistakenly cover irrelevant logs. Therefore, the logs of interest should be determined by request time duration collected based on practical transaction runtime. The runtime duration will be discussed later along with request tracing in Section 3.6.

To obtain densely distributed representation of transactions, the document representation approach from natural language processing is introduced [158]. The document distributed representation, called *doc2vec*, stems from word distributed representation [159], which is called *word2vec*. The word2vec succeeds in not only capturing word-level semantic meaning, but also adapting semantic transferring into word vector calculation. Furthermore, the doc2vec inherits the mechanism of word2vec to wrap up an extra paragraph or document vector to entail a *topic*.

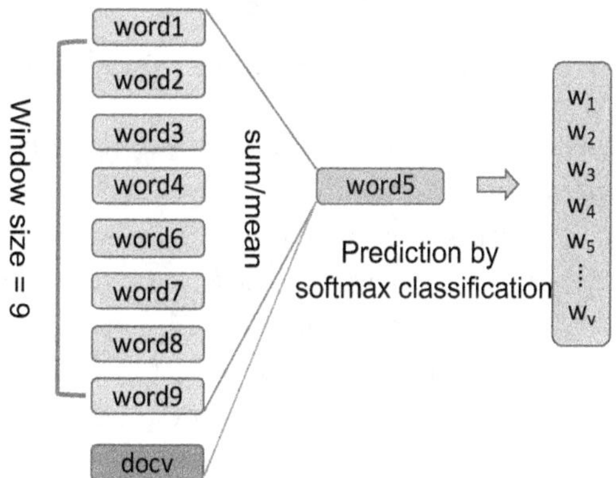

Fig. 3.2 Embedding Learning of Word2vec and Doc2vec

Generally, the word embedding learning refers to word2vec-like algorithms, learning distributed representation of text elements. From Fig. 3.2, it illustrates fundamental concepts of word2vec and the following doc2vec. To simplify the theory, the Continuous Bag of Words (CBOW) in [159] is introduced. The embedding learning attempts to converge each word vector within a time window by aggregating the context information and predicting the central word. At the beginning, each word will assign with an randomly initialized vector. Choosing a window size, e.g., *win* = 9, will constrain and determine the scope and context of interest. As shown in Fig. 3.2, *word5* takes the center position, hence being taken as prediction objective. The other 8 words make up the context information, which are aggregated by summing or averaging the vectors. The prediction is accomplished by softmax function with the input vector $w = (w_1, w_2, ..., w_v)$, where v is the size of the entire vocabulary. The window will slide through the entire sentence to ensure learning every words and each moving step produces a training example. On top of the CBOW paradigm, the doc2vec simply adds a fixed extra vector *docv* into training process. The basic idea is very similar except that *docv* is chosen identically across the sentence. Note that *docv* would not remain fixed in training but would keep using the same vector instance across window sliding.

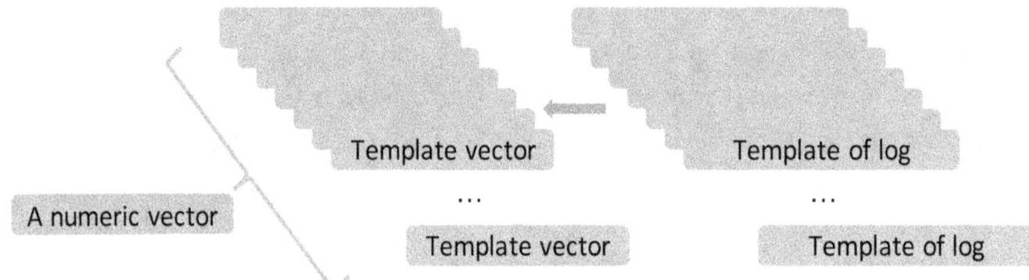

Fig. 3.3 Transaction Execution Behavior Representation

In contrast to intuitive and generic natural language processing, the model utilizes *doc2vec* over log template sentence-level rather than constant word-level. That is in the log analysis, the analysis grain is log templates rather than general language words. In essence, a language sentence can be seen as a sequence of words. Similarly, it is reasonable to imagine that a complete transaction or task is a sequence of meta-executions, printed by a sequence of logs that can be substituted by intrinsic templates. Thus, in log analysis, one template corresponds to one "word", and one transaction log collection corresponds to one "sentence". Then such a "sentence" (an actual transaction or task) is fed into a *doc2vec* model to learn its distributed vector representation. As can be seen from Fig. 3.3, each template is embedded as a template vector, and via *doc2vec* a sequence of log template is also embedded as a transaction embedding vector.

3.6 Service Query Tracing Representation Learning

This section depicts service tracing module to extract routine and subroutine response duration to construct the temporal information. Service tracing is of special interest in large scale and distributed server clusters as well as the microservices architecture, which couple each other with a communication mechanism, i.e., RESTful API. As a web-search example described in [160], the basic front-end functionality in distributed platforms heavily depend on frequent service queries, whose responses normally consist of a stable relation chain.

The targeted scenario is that user-oriented queries are sent from the very first front-end to all computation provider back-ends, which is inclined to form a spanned tree-like structure. The motivation is that if a complete query path can be well tracked, a malfunction action can be well identified and located. The "Dapper" tool depicted in [160] provides a robust, scalable and effective implementation as well as "Zipkin" in [161], and "Osprofiler" in [162]. Practically, a tracing component will insert a light weight collector into each service point, and immediately return service activities to central monitor. The light weight collectors should only cause negligible overhead and be transparent to application developers [160]. Fig. 3.4 illustrates service query chain, spanned as a tree structure.

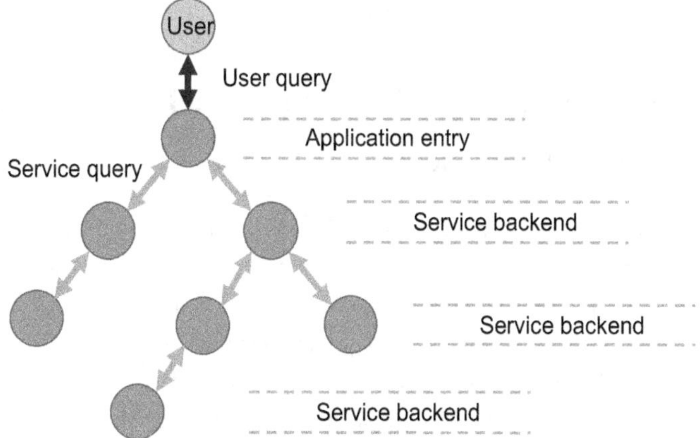

Fig. 3.4 A User Request from Front-end to Back-end Path

From Fig. 3.4, users launch a service request through an interface, the application entry. In the following, the request is processed as several parts which are delivered to back-end service point via service queries, as depicted as light blue arrows. It is possible that the first tier receiving queries merely conduct intermediate analysis so that first tier queries are mapped to the next service tier. Queries are eventually disassembled to multiple primitive ones, sent to the last tier, and results are reversely responded to the application entry, where all messages are assembled and replied to users. In this case, there are three levels of service back-end points.

In the proposed framework, the tracing infrastructure is utilized for structure-related information, because service requests and back-end queries durations implicitly reflect the function integrity. With the assistance of a tracing module, the whole query durations are stored to construct a service query matrix to record one transaction inner component query histories. Eq. 3.1 below shows a simple example of service query matrix. Here, services are denoted as numbered columns and rows. Columns are the query sender point and rows are the receivers. Each entry indicates the response duration from column to row. For instance, *Service Query Matrix*$(1,2) = 0.4$ means service 1 calling service 2 with response duration 0.4 seconds. The matrix explicitly contains all the necessary structural time information extracted from tracing module, and will combine its corresponding transaction "*topic*" vector as the complete temporal-spatial representation.

$$
\textit{Service Query Matrix} =
\begin{bmatrix}
0 & 2 & 0 & 0.1 & 0 \\
0.4 & 0 & 0.3 & 0 & 0 \\
0 & 0 & 0 & 0.78 & 1.7 \\
1.5 & 0 & 0.9 & 0 & 0 \\
0 & 1.1 & 0 & 0.33 & 0
\end{bmatrix}
\tag{3.1}
$$

3.7 Integrated Anomaly Detection Based on Temporal-Spatial Data Representation

Based on the behavior and query chain representation, extracted by doc2vec and tracing mechanism, respectively, the two parts should be integrated as an integrated feature vector. The feature vector will be taken as input to an anomaly detector.

For representation integration, firstly the matrix should be converted into a vector. In general, a matrix is flattened with respect to column or row. That is, for row, placing all rows elements in one single row but keeping their relative context position. In the following experiment, the service query matrix is flattened across row and the dimension is $dim_{query} = n \times n$, where n denote the number of services. To keep the dimension consistent through all data samples, the number is for the total service. In one transaction, it is possible that not all services are involved, in which case irrelevant columns and rows are set as 0. Afterwards, to aggregate two parts, transaction "*topic*" vector and service query vector can be concatenated seamlessly. The concatenation results in a hybrid vector with dimension $dim_{concat} = dim_{query} + dim_{log}$.

As for the anomaly detector, the basic idea is to absorb the features of normal samples and clarify the normality boundary in a feature space in training, and identify outliers in practice. Here, in training, all input samples are assumed normal and for test samples, outliers will be considered as anomalies against the normal sample distribution. One noteworthy issue is to confirm a proper high-dimensional area to encompass the training cluster. To this end, one-class classification (OCC) [163] is investigated, which is prevalent in anomaly detection sphere [163, 164]. Different from multi-classification, a challenge arises when there is little multiple categories knowledge in training dataset but aware of their similar characteristics. When there is an newly incoming data point, a classifier is able to highlight its belonging to training set or not. Several classic methods are belong to the OCC sphere, including the Local Outlier Factor algorithm [165], the Isolation Forest [166], One-class SVM [167, 168], clustering based detection [169]. From the OCC algorithms, the one-class support vector machine (OSVM) [167, 168] is of special interest. That is because in the integrated anomaly detection, there is no assumption on the distribution of joint spatial and temporal information. The representative log and trace information are apparently located in distinguished spaces without direct correlations, and the concatenation presents no evident clue on integration of original distributions. It can hardly draw the conclusion that density-related methods shall capture reasonable locality in the original data space. Nonetheless, one-class SVM shall expand or shrink its decision bound in higher dimensional spaces with the assistant of the kernel trick, which brings a chance to learn a reasonable bound of normal samples.

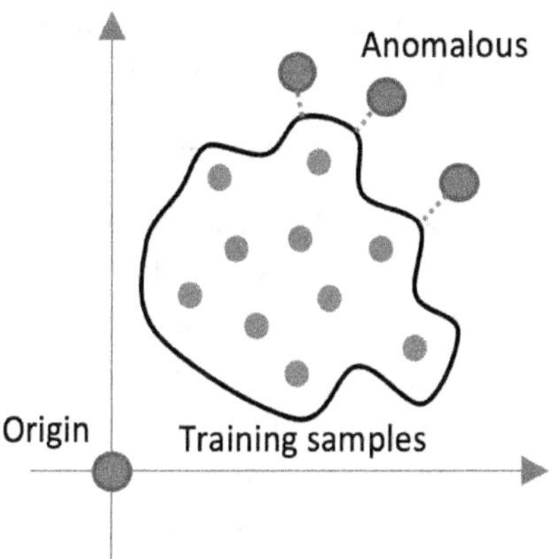

Fig. 3.5 A Case of The OSVM to Train Samples against The Origin

The OSVM adopts the similar idea to standard support vector machine, by drawing an optimal boundary to separate two types. In OSVM, only one category is specified, therefore the other one is formed by the origin in the feature space. Moreover, the OSVM essentially finds a least radius sphere in hyperplane to encompass training data, if using kernel trick for linear non-separable situation. As shown in Fig. 3.5, red circles denote training samples, which should be separated against the origin. Note that the boundary drawn is not a strict sphere in the 2D space, but remain spherical in a high dimensional space. The OSVM is robust to noise in training set since it mainly concentrates on flexible data distribution boundary, and the training is effective and fast given a small size of dataset. It is reasonable to consider the advantage of OSVM, provided that collectible and deterministic fault samples in a complex architecture. Therefore, we employ the OSVM algorithm as the outlier classifier to fit in small size training data and detect inserted transaction anomalies. Three blue-colored points are marked as anomalous due to their locations. The blue dash lines denote the distance from boundary to outliers.

3.8   Experiment Results and Analysis

In this section, we will present the empirical experiments of template extraction and integrated anomaly detection with concatenated features. The data processing machine is with 16-core Intel Xeon E5-2630 v3 CPU, 64GB memory, and Nvidia GTX 1080Ti GPU.

Table 3.1 Log Datasets in Experiments

Dataset	BlueGene/L		OpenStack	
Volume	Total 4,747,963		Total 269,169	
	Info/Warning	Error	Info/Warning	Error
	3,759,170	988,793	243,780	25,389

Data are from a public dataset and a distributed platform. The public dataset comes from the BlueGene/L [25], a supercomputer developed by IBM Watson Research Center. The BlueGene/L data will only be utilized in template extraction as there lacks high level transactional label and essential service tracing records for the tracing matrix. The OpenStack log data are collected from OpenStack services, i.e., nova-computing, neutron-networking, and etc., deployed in three physical computing nodes. As described before, we make use of Osprofiler, the OpenStack tracing module, to store hierarchical request trace paths. For evaluating anomaly detection, 122 user transaction samples are collected from virtual instance creation and deletion. All data are labeled as 100 normal samples, and 22 outliers, as well. As for labeling, once a request is sent into OpenStack, the trace module will start to construct a request tree via inserted probes and assign a unique trace ID to it. Aligning the ID and starting time, the corresponding logs are directly located.

Table 3.1 depicts the summary of the volume of two datasets. BlueGene/L contains more than 4 million logs in total, two thirds of which stay with "info" and "warning" severity. Similarly, OpenStack has nearly 270,000 records with most "info" and "warning" severity. In the chapter, the main object is these "info" and "warning" records. This is fairly reasonable, because the assumption is that if "error" appears, it surely points to an anomaly, however if

Table 3.2 Transactional Data Description

Log Volume		243,780	
Sample Volume	Total 122	Normal 100	Abnormal 22
Sample Type	Total 122	Creation 96	Deletion 26

only "info" and "warning" appear, abnormal events probably are hidden under the seemingly healthy records.

Table 3.2 describes the transaction sample dataset for high-level transaction representation learning and service tracing matrix construction. The first column indicates the data volume in terms of different situations: log volume refers to the total number of log events; sample volume refers to the division of tasks in terms of normality; sample type refers to the division of tasks in terms of task type. In total, 122 samples are collected, 100 normal samples and 22 abnormals, through basic virtual instance creation and deletion requested by user. Note that samples here are based on the task instances, each of which may contain numerous log events. In abnormal conditions, interferences have been inserted to make instance creation unsuccessful or long delay. Wherein, unsuccessful creation is triggered by not enough user quote, and the long delay is due to the broken physical networking. Note that the inadequate quote is not a system anomaly, but it still can be marked as failed request with "info" and "warning" records. The proposed model can successfully identify the exceptions.

3.8.1   Evaluation of Template Extraction

Table 3.3 Template Extraction Results

Method	Block Size	Accuracy	Time (s)
IPLoM		0.54	31.9
Segmented Iteration	10000	0.57	16.44
	100000	0.56	**12.26**
Elastic Aggregation	10000	0.53	16.92
	100000	**0.61**	12.38

In the beginning, the results show the efficiency and analyze the concrete outcomes of template extraction between IPLoM and the method. Some evaluations have been done in [34] and [35]. We take advantage of the open-source material with default setting for BlueGene/L logs and implement the proposed method in this Chapter. The parameter setting is: the information threshold, *Thr*, is set as 0.5 to keep at least 50% terms; the log count in one segment or buffered size in an on-line scheme, *Seg_interval*, is set as 10000, and 100000, respectively; furthermore, in the *long template adjustment*, the exceeding percentage is set as 0.9. The results are shown in Table 3.3. From the accuracy, the proposed method is competitive and even performs slightly better than the original IPLoM. The highest one is the elastic aggregation with accuracy 0.61. As for the time cost, both of the proposals are nearly as twice as faster than IPLoM.

3.8.2   Evaluation of Transactional Topic Representation

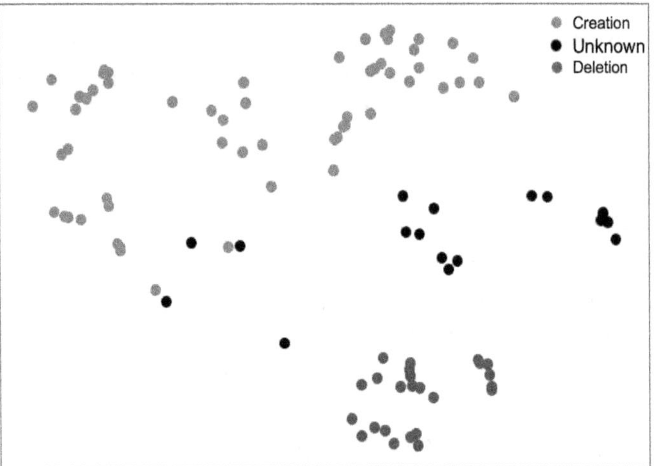

Fig. 3.6 Visualization of Transactional Representation

Following template extraction, the whole raw log messages are converted into their corresponding templates. Each transactional logs block is located by request time stamps labeled in tracing modules. The *doc2vec* algorithm takes as input the located normal transactional log blocks to train the *document* representation with $dim_{log} = 150$. A high dimension space needs to be visualized to verify its interpretability. To this end, the t-SNE algorithm [170] is adopted in Fig. 3.6 to map high dimensional representations into 2D space and properly visualize the space structure. Additionally, the DBSCAN method [36] clusters the normal samples into two groups, marked as red and blue, respectively. It is because two distinct tasks, instance creation and deletion, are included and their fine grain executions differ widely. In Fig. 3.6, the black circles are labeled as noisy by the DBSCAN in high dimension, and approximately formed a separation line between the two groups.

3.8.3 Evaluation of Tracing Representation

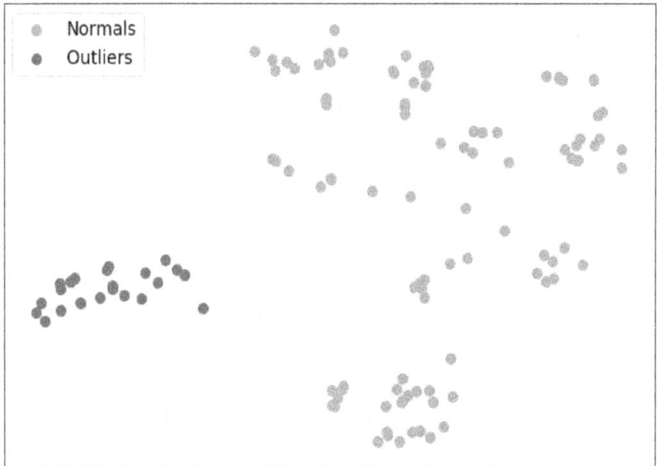

Fig. 3.7 Visualization of All Samples with Ground Truth Labels

The tracing mechanism recognizes 20 services in OpenStack, therefore one 20×20 trace matrix is flattened as a $dim_{query} = 400$ vector. Concatenated with *document* representation, the ultimate integrated vector is with $dim_{concat} = 550$. From Fig. 3.7, it illustrates all sample with ground truth labels distributed in 2D space through the t-SNE. The cyan blue circles are normal points, and the magenta circles refers to inserted abnormal requests. Obviously, the combined features clearly reflect the distinct cluster natures, which enables the following outlier classifier.

3.8.4 Evaluation of Anomaly Detection

By the OSVM method with radial basis function (RBF) kernel, the detection results are visualized in Fig. 3.8. As in Fig. 3.8, training with the normal data marked as cyan has 0.91 training accuracy and all anomalies are successfully identified, marked as magenta on the left. Compared to Fig. 3.7 above, several normal data are mistakenly identified as anomalies. It conjectures that in high dimensional training, these data are placed near the periphery of normal distribution boundary, though distant from anomalies. Without an elastic sphere boundary, possibly a small number of normals are segregated out of the normal scope.

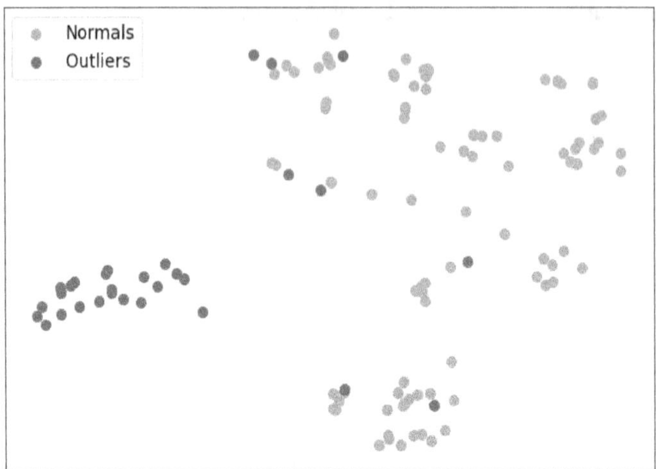

Fig. 3.8 Visualization of Anomaly Detection Labels

3.9 Summary

To conclude, the functional and transactional anomaly detection is crucial for efficient management and maintenance in a large-scale micro-services architecture. A general-purpose anomaly detection framework is proposed to target at micro-services architectures, using temporal service execution logs and spatial service query traces. The framework works compatibly with but not limited in *doc2vec* and *tracing matrix*. Experiment results have shown competitive performance and effectiveness of the proposed scheme: the template extraction achieves competitive accuracy and high efficiency; the transactional representation visualizes the distribution that samples entail; with the aid of spatial service query traces, the integrated representation segregates anomalies from normal points and helps the outlier classifier to highlight those anomalies.

Chapter 4

Network System Fault Localization and Ranking

4.1 Introduction

Previous work achieves anomaly detection of service-oriented networking architecture, and gains insightful results and decent performance. It is worth noting that the anomaly detection merely unveils labels or marks of high level events or predict the trends of them. One commonly accepted issue is that only learning a global label or a summary of an event is not sufficient for management. Identifying anomalies is the first step, followed by deeply and correctly localizing root cause and fault source, which is the step stone of fault prevention, solution and recovery. Localizing the root cause directly highlights the central issue raised by the anomaly and reveal the causality of service interaction. Localizing root cause also provides awareness in advance of anomaly details, becoming the key to prevent from catastrophic collapse.

This chapter considers the root cause localization problem as the core issue of networking diagnosis and proposes a ranking model to emphasize potential sources. On top of the networking anomaly detection outcomes, the localization focuses on digging out hidden relations between interconnected services and using the relations to infer the service significance and severity. The common wisdom of root cause analysis is offering a reasonable solution to a particular visible problem or a reported issue by a trouble ticket. For the localization of faults [171, 172], a probabilistic model should be built based on fault propagation to cover the networking system. In the context of the chapter, micro-services architecture root cause analysis, the aim is to point out the most suspicious service node rather than outputting descriptive technical summary.

4.2 Overview of Fault Localization Framework

To this end, a hierarchical ranking process is proposed. The process starts from transaction type filtering to service significance computing, followed by discrepancy calculation between actual time consumption and historical average, finally ending up with components ranking of a filtered task. The inputs of the process consist of the detected anomaly logs, the corresponding trace matrices and a newly constructed dependency matrix. The dependency matrix is based on calling links and is described in Section 4.5. There are three stages to accomplish it: 1) calculating anomaly degree and ranking the anomalous samples based on a sequential prediction model; 2) building an error matrix against history average; 3) calculating significance ratio vector with a dependency matrix based on PageRank and outputting the final suspicious ranking list. An overview of localization framework is presented in Fig. 4.1. Each red dotted frame illustrates a complete step. The black arrows cover the data-flow in the framework.

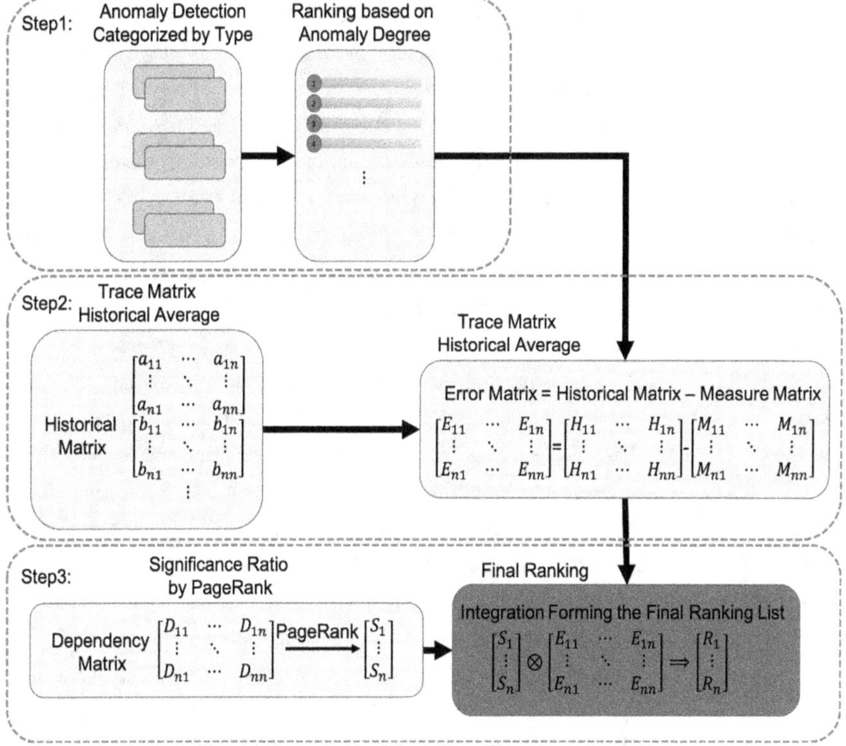

Fig. 4.1 Framework of Fault Root Cause Localization

Below, the anomaly degree is introduced in Section 4.3, followed by trace error matrix in Section 4.4, and lastly, localizing and ranking services in Section 4.5.

4.3   Ranking Based on Anomaly Degree

In this section, the first step is to filter the most anomalous individual request type. The assumption is that during a period of interest, various kinds of user requests launch the corresponding systematic transactions or tasks, and a number of anomalies occur as well. The hypothesis is that the root causes always hide in the most notable anomalies. As such, the job is to find out which anomaly or the type of anomalies is the most representative and reflects the most symptoms.

In light of the anomaly detection outcomes in Chapter 3, it is reasonable to stem the anomaly degree from the detected abnormal samples instead of normal samples. The anomalous samples would hold fault representative information that could lead to track down to the problem source. In complicated systems, a single true fault always triggers numerous visible error signs across relevant complete tasks, for instance, massive printed error and fatal severity logs, unexpected work-flows and excessively long processing delays. Furthermore, if a functional node provides a core service for one type of tasks and is experiencing an erroneous operation, the type of tasks will surely have serious and exterior symptoms. On the contrary, if a functional node imposes less heavily on a type of tasks, the visible symptoms are likely to barely presents low severity. Even if a service is excluded from a task request, the relevance is highly possible reduced to none. The above observation supports the localization hypothesis and shows the right direction to implement it.

The following problem becomes how to determine the anomaly degree based on the recognized tasks. Here, one sequential model is utilized to capture log data temporal characteristics. A basic assumption is that before anomaly identification, normal samples are collected for training a baseline, as the outlier classifier training in Chapter 3. The sequential model is fitted with the normal collected log data in training phase and in testing phase, incoming stream log data are evaluated and checked in matching. The adopted sequential model is one of the Recurrent Neural Networks (RNN) models, Long Short Term Memory (LSTM) [173]. The detail will be elucidated below.

The RNN model prevails in sequential data analysis in deep learning community [92] and can be visualized in Fig. 4.2. From Fig. 4.2, x_t, o_t, and s_t denote input data, output data and hidden state, respectively. The time index conforms to $0 < t < \infty$, and the practical range will be within a sequence of interest. The input x_t is the representation of log templates learned by word embedding [101] as the same as transactional representational learning. The templates remain the same order as the raw logs and the sequential data are turned into a sequence of distributed vectors as the time series input of the RNN. The outputs also construct a sequence that should match a given sequence of labels to guide the neural networks training direction. Generally, an input sequence and its labels pair is called a training pair. A conventional way to accomplish it is shifting a input sequence forward one time step to be its output labels.

As for the cell, it is the processing core of RNN which transforms input data into the implicit forms (hidden state s_t) in a high-dimensional vector space, and is capable of projecting the implicit forms into output representation. The left red dotted rectangle covers the unrolled structure of the RNN and the right rectangle reveals one cell unit recurrently wraps up the previous hidden state to merge into the current processing.

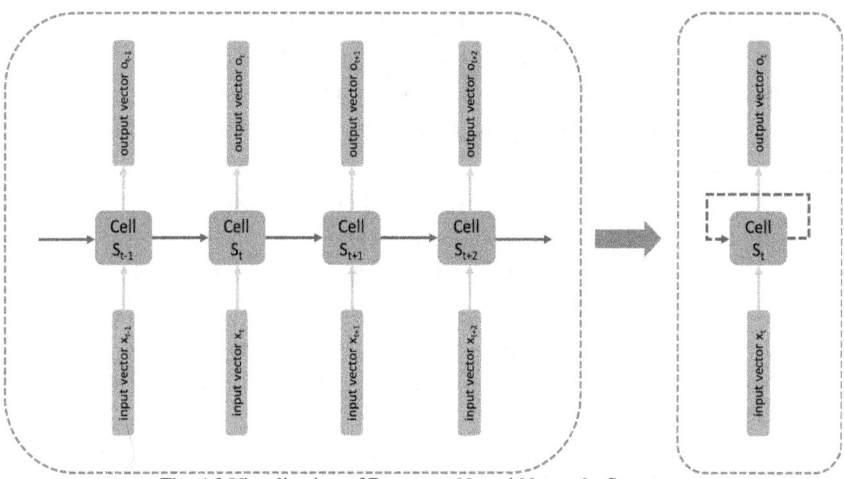

Fig. 4.2 Visualization of Recurrent Neural Networks Structure

The formulation of the RNN can be defined as below:

$$s_t = f_{cell}(x_t) \tag{4.1}$$

$$o_t = f_{out}(s_t) \tag{4.2}$$

In Eq. 4.6, the cell function passes x_t at step t to compress into the hidden state s_t, and Eq 4.2 transforms the hidden state s_t into o_t. Here, t is consistent with the concept in Fig. 4.2, whose range is within a sequence of interest. In effect, f_{cell} is chosen as a Hyperbolic function *tanh* in original RNN, while in LSTM cell, the f_{cell} is divided as three processing gates: the input gate determines how much input information should be received; the forget gate determines how much history information should be omitted; the output gate determines how much current information should be outputted. The LSTM is formulated in the following:

$$f_i = G_f(x_t, s_{t-1}) \tag{4.3}$$

$$i_t = G_i(x_t, s_{t-1}) \tag{4.4}$$

$$o_t = G_o(x_t, s_{t-1}) \tag{4.5}$$

$$c_t = Cell(c_{t-1}, x_t, i_t, f_t, s_{t-1}) \tag{4.6}$$

$$h_t = State(o_t, c_t) \tag{4.7}$$

In Eq. 4.3, Eq. 4.4, and Eq. 4.5, the gate functions G are Sigmoid functions, containing three groups of parameters for forget gate, information gate and output gate, respectively. Different from the original RNN, LSTM has a cell state c_t that helps store sequence relations. Then, the outputs are obtained directly from the output gate. Furthermore, for complex data structure, standard LSTM models can be stacked to enhance the capacity of capturing complex regularity. In this chapter, two LSTM blocks are stacked and the stacked entity is called a two-layer LSTM model.

As such, the two-layer LSTM model is employed to learn sequential characteristics from a sequence of extracted log template data of normal tasks. A well trained LSTM model is then utilized to compute the anomaly degree of one anomalous sample. The idea is that the LSTM model attempts to predict the future templates that are compared with ground truth in an anomalous sample. The prediction basically outputs a list of the top likely results. The comparison is to match the ground truth with the list position and the anomaly degree is exponential to the matched position.

Eq. 4.8 formulates the sequential model and its *top-m* list $list_{o_t}^{(m)}$, where o_t denotes the template at time step t, and $o_{0:t-1}$ denotes the previous templates as a time series from step 0 to $t-1$. In Eq. 4.9, if the template label l_t belongs to the $list_{o_t}^{(m)}$, the corresponding positioning Pos_{l_t} is recorded by an argument search function $f_{arg}(\cdot)$, otherwise, the positioning is assigned by $m+1$. The positioning Pos_{l_t} is subsequently subtracted by m in an exponential expression in Eq. 4.10 to compute how anomalous the template is at time t, which is called anomaly degree.

$$list_{o_t}^{(m)} = SeqModel(o_{0:t-1}) \tag{4.8}$$

$$Pos_{l_t} = \begin{cases} f_{arg}(list_{o_t}^{(m)}, l_t), & \text{if } l_t \in list_{o_t}^{(m)} \\ m+1, & \text{otherwise} \end{cases} \tag{4.9}$$

$$Dgr = exp(Pos_{l_t} - m) \tag{4.10}$$

Here, the degree *Dgr* records merely individual template status. For a complete task, all individual templates should be aggregated. The aggregation could be based on *sum* and *mean*. *sum* focuses on ensemble degree of the entire task, while *mean* emphasizes the average individual capacity. In addition to task-level, multiple tasks of the same type could occur within one time-window, for which the anomaly degree in terms of type level should be carefully considered as well. In this chapter, *mean* is adopted in task-level degree aggregation to relief long log sequence bias and *sum* is adopted in type-level degree aggregation to highlight the most significant occurrence.

4.4 Trace Error Matrix and Dependency matrix

In this section, we will introduce the trace error matrix (TEM) for finding the most noticeable query duration discrepancy and the dependency matrix (DM) for subsequent PageRank calculation. Both of the TEM and the DM stem from the service query tracing module depicted in Chapter 3. The TEM is obtained by calculating service history trend and the DM is obtained by querying frequency.

From Chapter 3, the service query trace matrix only captures single transaction structure information for systematic representation. Nevertheless, service querying features have not been fully leveraged for in-depth mining. The individual spatial information merely reflects discrete and possibly exceptional features, which are utilized in an abstract way in anomaly detection. In localization, knowledge should be narrowed down to element-wise analysis in order to highlight suspicious services.

An intuitive idea is to reveal the discrepancy between the actual observations and the history trend, afterwards denoted by *Trace Error Matrix*. The discrepancy, also called *Trace Error Matrix*, can directly measure which part has been changed the most when an anomaly occurs. Thus, the history trends construct a baseline of each querying duration in normal operation over collected transactional traces, which can be accomplished by element-wise averaging tracing query matrix, i.e., simple average, moving average and exponential moving average. The three averaging methods implement three perspectives of history trends: the simple average makes efforts to consider the overall service performance; the moving average pays more attention to recent sample information with respect to history time labels; lastly, the exponential moving average attempts to assign temporal importance to the recent samples of special interests. Eq. 4.11 and Eq. 4.12 formulate the calculation of the TEM.

$$TEM = M_{obs} - M_{trend} \qquad (4.11)$$

$$M_{trend} = F_{avg}(M_{sample}) \tag{4.12}$$

where M_{obs} is the service query matrix of a detected sample and M_{sample} denotes history normal data. As for $F_{avg}(\cdot)$,

$$
F_{avg}(\cdot) = \frac{1}{N}\sum_{0}^{N} M^{t}_{sample} \qquad \text{sample average for } N \text{ samples}
$$

$$
= \frac{1}{n}\sum_{t-n}^{t} M^{t}_{sample} \qquad \text{moving average in } n \text{ steps}
$$

$$
= \begin{cases} M^{t}_{sample}, & \text{if } t = 1 \\ \delta \cdot M^{t}_{sample} + (1-\delta) \cdot F^{t-1}_{avg} \end{cases} \qquad \text{exponential moving average}
$$

When an anomaly is detected, its actual observation matrix is subtracted by the history trend to obtain the eventual *Trace Error Matrix*. The *Trace Error Matrix* will be regarded as the actual anomalous status fused with inherent significance to capture the most suspicious component.

Unlike the *Trace Error Matrix*, the *Dependency Matrix* captures the calling procedures rather than actual response durations, which will lack the temporal information but hold the service interaction relations. An intriguing perspective is that the entire dependency process corresponds to a topology-like graph where each node is an independent service and each link is built by the calling connection. In the following, a topology-like graph is mathematically modeled as a matrix. In detail, the row and column settings are the same as the *Trace Error Matrix*, and the entries store the interaction frequency. Originally, the service tracing module collects the calling counts from an individual front-end service to each one of its back-end services during one specific type of task. In the original *Dependency Matrix*, the entries are the collected request counts. From the perspective of functionality and utility, the calling information directly reflects the importance of each individual service in the running task. If a service is activated with a large amount of requests, it is apparently supposed to maintain a key element for completing the whole process. It therefore discovers a service occupying an important position during the task. Furthermore, the relative significance is of interest instead of the absolute summed count. The significance is then represented as probability weights that are normalized by the overall callings, which can be regarded as the task state quasi-transition probabilities in this regard. As such, the original *Dependency Matrix* is converted based on the probability weights to eventually construct a Markov matrix [174]. The quasi-transition *Dependency Matrix* will be utilized to calculate the inherent significance of each service with respect to each type of tasks.

Though the *Trace Error Matrix* and *Dependency Matrix* are distinctive from the process of construction, they in fact wrap up two facets of the systematic service request-response mechanism. The *Trace Error Matrix* flexibly extracts the explicit discrepancy between the history trend and the current suspicious sample. In the meantime, the *Dependency Matrix* implicitly extracts the static and intrinsic relations that are based on the ideology of designing. Both of the two matrices are jointly leveraged in the following Section for highlighting and localizing the most serious service point in the system.

4.5   Localizing Services by Significance Ranking

The *Trace Error Matrix* reflects the actual discrepancy incurred by each component in the runtime. It is a naive approach to sort out the root cause within one operation. Nonetheless, each component may present a symptom without inherent importance. That is the *Trace Error Matrix* measures the error seriousness in one single operation regardless of corresponding service weights in this request type. For instance, in a cloud platform, creation of virtual machine involves in the same classes of back-end services as migration of virtual machine, while creation instead of migration tends to access the image management module frequently in the beginning. The importance of each service is likely to be distinctive for various tasks in this regard.

In fact, for each type of task, there exists an inherent significance assignment since the corresponding service functions were designed and developed. On top of the type of a forthcoming task, system will automatically determine what back-end services will be invoked and in what order these services respond. In many cases, a service may not have only one back-end support and in turn, a service may have to answer to multiple front-end requests during one single task. An obvious phenomenon is that the more front-end services calling one particular back-end point, the more crucial it is likely to be to the completeness and performance of functionality. A topology-like graph properly fits the complicated query-response relations and expresses the whole structure in an explicit mathematical matrix.

A simplified topology-like dependence graph is presented in Fig. 4.3. In this figure, the circles represent one functional service point in a system, and the arrows represent back-end service querying links. There are three tracing layers, front-end services, mid-layer services and the last level back-end services, respectively. In the beginning, users post requests for tasks of interests, and these requests are forwarded to the front-end services. The front-end services ingest the primitive request and resolve them as several sub-tasks that are distributed to some corresponding lower layer servicing points to process. The mid-layer services receive the sub-tasks and further disassemble them into meta-queries that will be delivered to the last servicing layer. The final back-end services only take configurations, data, and objects as input and respond to the tasks binded predecessors. In Fig. 4.3, arrows with the same color and style are belong to the same tasks. It is manifest from Fig. 4.3 that each front-end service can send multiple services to one descendant and in turn each mid-layer and back-end service can ingest multiple queries from different predecessors. Additionally, a user request can declare more than one front-end services to jointly accomplish it as shown with the circles linked by dotted green arrows.

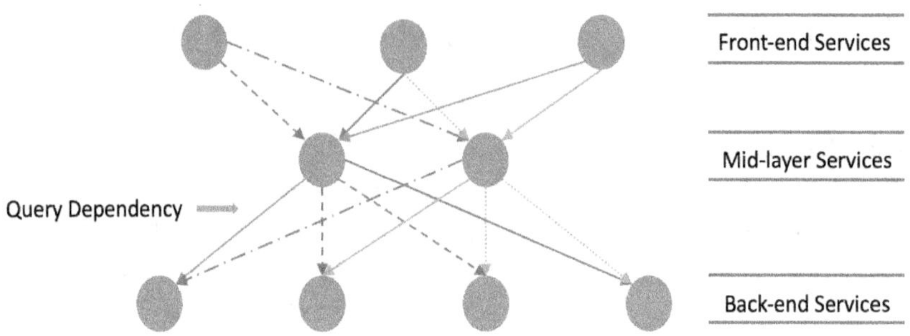

Fig. 4.3 Tracing Graph Based on Systematic Query Dependence

The aforementioned *Dependence Matrix* shows an opportunity to capture the fundamental significance of individual services despite it is instantiated as a sparse correlation matrix. The above graph is adopted to construct a 9×9 dependence matrix, each entry of which is obtained by the invocation frequency from row services to column services. Hence, the PageRank algorithm [175] is introduced to compress the interaction information into dense importance representation.

The PageRank algorithm was proposed in the context of web applications and services, which offered an effective way to determine the importance of an accessible web page. It was firstly employed for the web search engines that returned a set of key word matched pages. The matched pages are all relevant to the real intension of users, however should be prompted in a reasonable order. The order is ranked based on a score measuring the importance or popularity of the web content in this regard. The results that top the ordered list has large chances to become the items of interests. As for the score, the PageRank algorithm would assign an initial weight to each accessible node in the graph and the weights are equal at the beginning. Links that direct one node to another refer to the dynamic score distributing or state-like transferring from perspective of system state representation. In the meanwhile, the entire graph completes a closed loop where each node gives out its score to descendants but receives scores from its predecessors. The closed loop reveals an iterative process and requires a convergence condition that guarantees fixed and stable scores after a limited iteration steps regardless of the initialized values. The convergence condition is that the transferring matrix embedded in the graph is a Markov matrix, which means either the column or the row vectors are stochastic vectors.

The *Dependence Matrix* perfectly fits in the PageRank algorithm requirement. The column vectors of the *Dependence Matrix* are inherently stochastic vectors, Since the original calling counts entries in the matrix are all recomputed as normalized service queries dependence weights. Analogous to the state transferring scenario, the nature of the *Dependence Matrix* can be viewed as operational state dynamics for a high level user request. The PageRank algorithm takes as input the *Dependence Matrix* to iteratively converge to a weight vector, in which each element corresponds to one working service revealing the inherent importance. The inherent importance is stable and only based on the system design ideology and functionality, while it is not explicitly provided. As such, it requires the PageRank method to achieve this.

The ultimate outcomes are forged by the *Trace Error Matrix* and services PageRank values as formulated at Eq. 4.13, where $\times$ denotes matrix product by a matrix and a vector. Here, the $\vec{l}$ is the final ranking value list that can be sorted to find the most suspicious node. *TEM* refers to *Trace Error Matrix* and $\vec{P_v}$ denotes the systematic default PageRank values of all existing active services. This can summarize the total error degrees in a particular task weighted by each service inherent importance. Apparently, the largest error indicates the largest gap between the normal baseline and the actual data.

$$\vec{l} = TEM \times \vec{P_v} \qquad\qquad (4.13)$$

4.6 Experiments

In this section, the settings of experiments are described to present the availability and feasibility of anomaly degree, instances of *Trace Error Matrix* and *Dependence*, and the ranking localization based on the PageRank algorithm. Firstly, we have overview of the experiment scenario. The process is consistent with the proposal framework in Fig. 4.1. The target micro-services platform is OpenStack with four fundamental components interacted with each other, as presented in Fig. 4.4. The green arrows denote that interactions direct to end users and the red arrows denote intra-queries. It is clear that the user requests are straightforward from the front-end. When there is an instance creation operation, the request is divided into several downstream queries: authentication, instance image retrieval, computing resource allocation and networking resource allocation. The operation and its order are recorded by the event logging module and the tracing management module, which provides abundant information for dependency analysis.

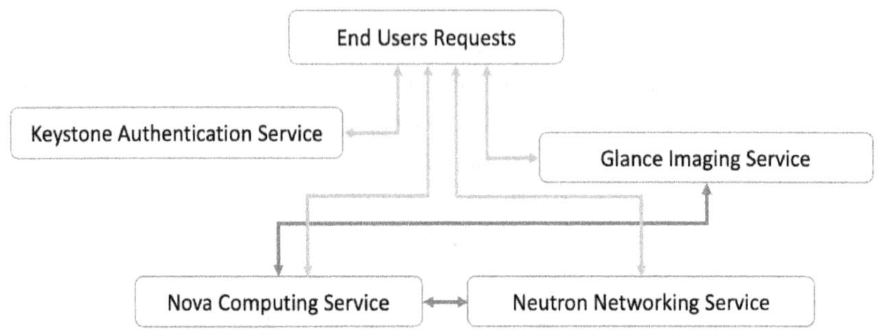

Fig. 4.4 The Topological Interaction with Each Fundamental Services

4.6.1 Experimental Environment and Data

As detailed depicted in Chapter 3, the localization conforms to the networking data process paradigm with representation and fusion. In this section, the experiment environment is still based on OpenStack cloud computing system with the tracing module, Osprofiler [162]. The functionality of Osprofiler is similar to that of Zipkin [161], the Dapper Tracing tool [160] from Google and other academic and industrial contributions [176–179].

In Chapter 3, the tracing module is employed to probe the actual servicing time to represent the systematic spatial information. However, as aforementioned, the drawback of pure servicing duration is shielding the correlation of each service node so that the root cause of a fault is difficult to highlight. With the assistance of the tracing module, the *Dependence Matrix* is extracted based on the query occurrence in a task. In addition, the *Service Tracing Matrix* of normal tasks are averaged to the historical normal operation baseline for the building of *Trace Error Matrix*. Besides the tracing information, the log data are the same as Chapter 3, while they are all transformed into symbolic sequences for sequential model construction. In normal tasks, the samples are collected based on instance creation and deletion, in the meanwhile the abnormal samples are collected based on the virtual instance creation.

4.6.2 Anomaly Degree Analysis

In Section 4.3, the RNN-augmented (LSTM) model block is introduced to memorize the sequential relations entailed in log sequences. The logs are preprocessed into the corresponding templates and its mark number in the template ''vocabulary'', the size of which is determined the amount the unique templates. The sequential model adopts 2-layer bi-directional LSTM with 512 units in hidden states and 256 units in log template embedding matrix. The unrolled sequence window is 10, predicting the template sequence of 1 time slot right-shifting.

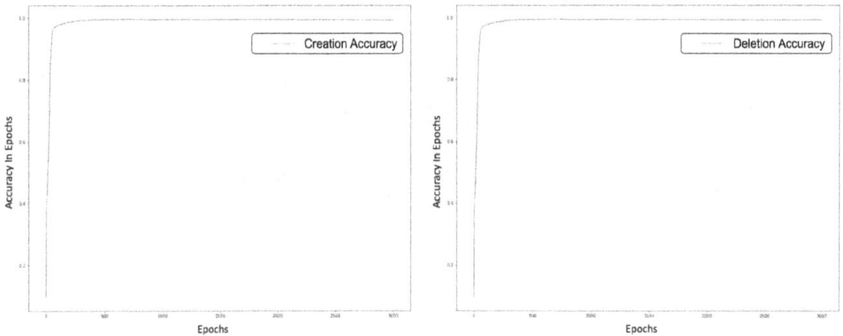

(a) Normal Instance Creation Task Samples   (b) Normal Instance Deletion Task Samples
Fig. 4.5 The Training Accuracy of Normal Instance Creation and Deletion Task Samples

It is clear from the Fig. 4.5, both of the training accuracy curves are very similar and converge fast, showing the capability of capturing the sequential features of logs across various types of tasks. Both of the training process of the instance creation and deletion task converge to the optimal parameter setting barely after 200 epochs though there carrying on 3000 epochs. The well-trained models are stored for the forthcoming anomaly degree calculation at different time checkpoints, i.e., 1000 epochs, 2000 epochs and 3000 epochs. Section 4.3 elucidates the anomaly degree formulation, which is an exponential expression based on the next template token prediction position. To explicitly illustrate the anomaly trend, the anomaly degree is computed by moving average with the triangle window type.

In Fig. 4.6, the left sub-graph and right sub-graph are the anomaly degree trends of instance creation samples and instance deletion samples, respectively. It is manifest from Fig. 4.6 that the anomaly degree trends of all the historical normal tasks remain close to 0. Although there exits an exception at the beginning prediction, it plunges to the low value within a very short period. It is worth noting that the degree calculation results are very similar nonetheless they are respectively compatible with a creation model and a deletion model. The model are divided based on the task types and will be loaded with the optimal performance checkpoint to apply to the collected datasets.

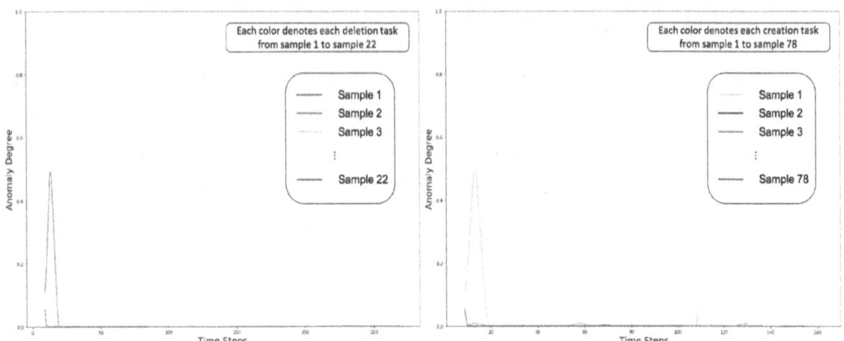

(a) Normal Instance Creation Task Samples   (b) Normal Instance Deletion Task Samples

Fig. 4.6 The Anomaly Degree of Normal Instance Creation and Deletion Task Samples

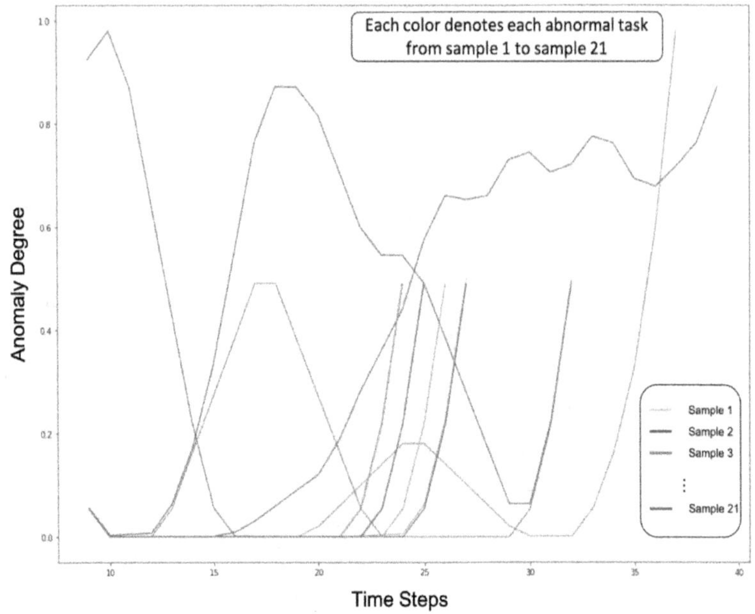

Fig. 4.7 The Anomaly Degree of Abnormal Instance Creation Task Samples

In contrast to the normal samples, Fig. 4.7, all the trends of instance creation task samples keep high values, most of which indicate the incremental trend. The abnormal testing data are all based on instance creation, therefore the loaded model is from well-trained instance creation checkpoint. The high anomaly degree values and the incremental trends compared to the normal samples evidently proves that the features of network faults and anomalies leave strong brands and fingerprints in the temporal log sequences. Also, the anomaly degree numerical values offer an effective measure to rank the most suspicious task type for the following service node-level root cause ranking and localization.

4.6.3 The Root Cause Analysis

To localize and rank the root cause of network anomalies and faults, the *Trace Error Matrix* is forged and combined with service PageRank values to obtain the most suspicious nodes. The PageRank values are calculated on top of the *Dependence Matrix* and listed for two types of tasks in Table 4.1. The service name not only contains the necessary components dedicated to the OpenStack functionality, but also records the physical host servers, e.g., *HPC-Lab01*. The communication mechanisms for service queries are additionally wrapped up as *rpc*, *neutron_api*, and *wsgi* etc. Note that there is a term named "*TopReq*", which refers to the user request entry point. The request entry for a user is like a general service node so that the entry is supposed to be part of the tracing. In an OpenStack system, there will be a master server for high level management and several slave servers for conveying virtual machines. In the experiment, the master server is appointed to the *HPC-Lab01* host therefore services like *nova-conductor*, and *nova-scheduler* are located at *HPC-Lab01*.

As for the values of PageRanks, the results are the average values of all creation tasks and deletion tasks. In fact, the PageRank values are different across tasks even belonging to the same type. It is because the virtual instance creation operations are probably allocated in different physical machines based on an OpenStack default resource management strategy. Since nova-compute service in OpenStack is responsible for computing resource management, each of physical machines has a service end point with a relatively high PageRank value.

Besides the PageRank value, the *Trace Error Matrix* stems from the tracing information of history normal operation baseline and the detected anomaly ones. Following the anomaly and faults detection in Chapter 3, the root causes are localized among the detected anomalous samples. The amount of services counts 20 from Table 4.1, making the baseline tracing matrix size 20×20 as well as the *Trace Error Matrix*. Both of the two types of matrix are sparse because one service only interacts with a few of others.

In Table 4.1, the final *Ranking Value* column presents a ranking list of a creation example. The true cause of the creation task failure is due to inadequate user instance quotes. Note that the issues of inadequate user instance is not a system problem but can be detected as in Chapter 3 and the root cause ranking value still gives insights of the issue source. The largest two service nodes are *rpc:nova:nova-conductor:HPC-Lab01* and *rpc:nova:nova-scheduler:HPC-Lab01*, respectively. The *nova-conductor* service enables OpenStack access the database and the *nova-scheduler* serves as the core instance launch decision agent. It is

Table 4.1 OpenStack Services and PageRank Values

Service Name	Creation	Deletion	Ranking Value
nova_image:nova:osapi_compute:HPC-Lab01	0.0102	0.0075	0.0219
vif_driver:nova:nova-compute:HPC-Lab01	0.0102	0.0075	0.0717
compute_api:nova:osapi_compute:HPC-Lab01	0.0303	0.0497	0.0379
rpc:nova:nova-conductor:HPC-Lab01	0.0666	0.0075	0.2306
wsgi:glance:api:HPC-Lab01	0.0095	0.0075	0.0188
rpc:nova:osapi_compute:HPC-Lab01	0.0075	0.0496	0
neutron_api:nova:nova-compute:HPC-Lab03	0.0113	0.0168	0.0398
neutron_api:nova:nova-compute:HPC-Lab01	0.0172	0.0241	0.0787
rpc:nova:nova-compute:HPC-Lab01	0.0616	0.0402	0.1281
wsgi:keystone:admin:HPC-Lab01	0.0075	0.0075	0.0379
rpc:nova:nova-scheduler:HPC-Lab01	0.0075	0.0075	0.2003
TopReq	0.0385	0.0588	0.0300
rpc:nova:nova-consoleauth:HPC-Lab01	0.0075	0.0075	0
neutron_api:nova:nova-compute:HPC-Lab02	0.0141	0.0197	0.0577
neutron_api:nova:osapi_compute:HPC-Lab01	0.0280	0.0277	0.0341
wsgi:nova:osapi_compute:HPC-Lab01	0.0252	0.0548	0.0143
rpc:nova:nova-compute:HPC-Lab03	0.0285	0.0229	0.0951
vif_driver:nova:nova-compute:HPC-Lab03	0.0085	0.0075	0.0371
rpc:nova:nova-compute:HPC-Lab02	0.0437	0.0282	0.1102
vif_driver:nova:nova-compute:HPC-Lab02	0.0093	0.0075	0.0530

reasonable to emphasize the database access point since the system validation mechanism attempts to hold the process from an invalid request. Though the *nova-scheduler* carries a low PageRank value, the inadequate quote issue prevents the scheduler from distributing the launch instructions, which dramatically raises the error gap and highlights the final ranking value.

4.7　Summary

In this chapter, we describe the framework of network anomaly and fault root cause localization by presenting sequential model anomaly degree prediction, *Trace Error Matrix* and *Dependence Matrix* construction, and the information fusion-based ranking value computation. Experiments of sequential model training process and localization ranking based on the collected task samples show that the proposed framework performs well and successfully captures core temporal and spatial information to provide interpretable insight of the abnormal issues.

Chapter 5

Network Traffic Resource Management

5.1   Introduction

Path planning is one of the most important aspects of TE, providing selected routing and forwarding paths between nodes to offer high-performance networks [180, 181]. Due to diversified services and advanced networking techniques like network virtualization, network dynamics have become a normal phenomenon, resulting in an increasing demand for path planning under various requirements and/or conditions [181–184]. For instance, forwarding path is restricted to go through one or several given nodes for e.g. traffic monitoring.

The emerging Software Defined Networking (SDN) paradigm [118, 185] has gained its popularity and drawn considerable attentions for smooth and rapid development of new TE algorithms, due to its capability of decoupling the control plane from the data plane. This decoupling releases computing resources in commodity switches to simplify switch functions and pull the forwarding decision making and computing into a high level controller, which is able to take global information into consideration.

With the increment of various emerging applications, massive data has been produced from the Internet [186, 110]. The hidden information behind the data implies important knowledge [187] for efficient TE [9]. Data-driven applications take as input the massive data to help adapt learning algorithms into distinctive circumstances. Successes in [188, 189] clarify the importance of leveraging useful data generated from the network. Their large-scale data analysis enables promising applications, such as semantic interpretation and user experience improvement.

The intention is to extend data-driven learning promoted by deep learning methods to the path planning problem. Deep learning has been massively developed and rapidly deployed by a variety of applications [92], which makes the utmost data be fully perceived by the application. Though deep learning methods have succeeded in many fields, challenges still exist when being introduced into network applications [9]. For example, dynamics in networking needs human-like behavior for model to fit.

To make a further progress, this chapter aims to have finer-grained network-level path planning driven by empirical traffic data. To achieve this purpose, we treat the network path as a sequential data, since a path with a set of forwarding hops explicitly express its serializability. One notable sequence analysis technique comes from Natural Language Processing (NLP), where sentences or phrases are intrinsically serialized. Inspired by sentences analysis in NLP, the proposal merges neural networks and build a sequence-to-sequence (seq2seq) model [190] to capture inner characteristics of sequence-like traffic forwarding and routing path. Abundant traffic information from the network can provide a natural way for model training. The method will extract sequential features from empirical traffic data and apply them into path discovery.

5.2   The Proposed Framework

This study aims to propose a forwarding method based on seq2seq model for path planning between two nodes, through learning common paths in a network from historical forwarding experiences.

5.2.1   Problem formulation

For the sake of clarity, Definition 5.2.1 is first given in this section.

Definition 5.2.1. The source sequence and target sequence are two network paths between source node and destination node. Each of them contains a set of network nodes to be traversed from source to destination.

The problem considered here is that, given the source sequence and constrained condition, it is going to find the target sequence which satisfies the constrained condition. For example, a source sequence can be (source, node 1, node 2, ..., node n, destination), and a constrained condition is that this network path need go through a particular node k. The target sequence is therefore (source, node 1, node 2, ..., node k, ..., node n, destination).

For clarity, it denotes source and target sequences as bold vector $\vec{\mathbf{x}}, \vec{\mathbf{y}}$, where $\vec{\mathbf{x}} = (x_1, x_2, ..., x_{n_x})$ with length n_x and $\vec{\mathbf{y}} = (y_1, y_2, ..., y_{n_y})$ with length n_y. The lower case letter x, y represent the element in a sequence.

5.2.2   The Inspired Forwarding Path Model

Fig. 5.1 provides a high-level illustration of the inspired forwarding method based on seq2seq model. An intuitive idea is that path generation can be deemed as a transformation from request sequences to ultimate sequences, which fits well in the seq2seq model. The scenario incorporates encoder-decoder into the SDN architecture, where the programmable switches in the data plane will conduct rules from a controller. The learning-based framework serves as an intelligent agent making decisions and deploying rules. The input sources are data transferring requests with constrains and the output shall be practical transferring paths corresponding to requests. The *Encoder* takes the source sequence as input and produces hidden states that are fed into the *Decoder* and the *Attention* (used to ensure reasonable order of nodes in a sequence). The *Decoder* receives the last hidden state from the *Encoder* to produce its own hidden states which are fed into the *Beam search* (used to enhance the performance of the proposed model) and back to the *Attention*, as the dashed arrow shows. The *Attention* scores the relevance between the hidden states of the *Encoder* and the *Decoder* to output context vectors. Eventually, the context vectors are jointly fed into the beam search with the hidden states of the *Decoder*, which is represented by the *addition* icon in the figure. The details of *Encoder* and *Decoder* have been illustrated in Section 5.3.2, and the details of *Attention* and *Beam search* will be elaborated in Sections 5.3.4 and 5.3.5.

Let θ, ω represent parameters and weights in neural networks, and let the capital letter $\mathscr{D}_s, \mathscr{D}_t$ denote the dataset of source sequence and target sequence, respectively. The number of elements in $\mathscr{D}_s$ and $\mathscr{D}_t$ is k.

As described in Section 5.3.2, it has the form of *Encoder* below:

$$\overrightarrow{\mathbf{m}_i} = En(\overrightarrow{\mathbf{x}_i}, \theta), \quad \overrightarrow{\mathbf{x}_i} \in \mathscr{D}_s, \quad i = 1,2,3,...,k \tag{5.1}$$

where $\overrightarrow{\mathbf{x}_i}$ is one of k elements in the dataset $\mathscr{D}_s$, and θ is the parameters of *Encoder*.

The source sequence is encoded into a fixed-length (dimension) vector as an intermedia sequence to bridge the gap (in terms of the number of network nodes) between a source sequence and a target sequence.

Equivalently, the *Decoder* can be given by:

$$y_i^j = De(\overrightarrow{\mathbf{y}_i^{-j}}, \omega | \overrightarrow{\mathbf{m}_i}), \quad \overrightarrow{\mathbf{y}_i} \in \mathscr{D}_t, \\ i = 1,2,3,...,k, \quad j = 1,2,3,...,n_y \tag{5.2}$$

where $-j$ indicates a sub-sequence $(y_1, y_2, ..., y_{j-1})$ of $\overrightarrow{\mathbf{y}_i}$ before t.

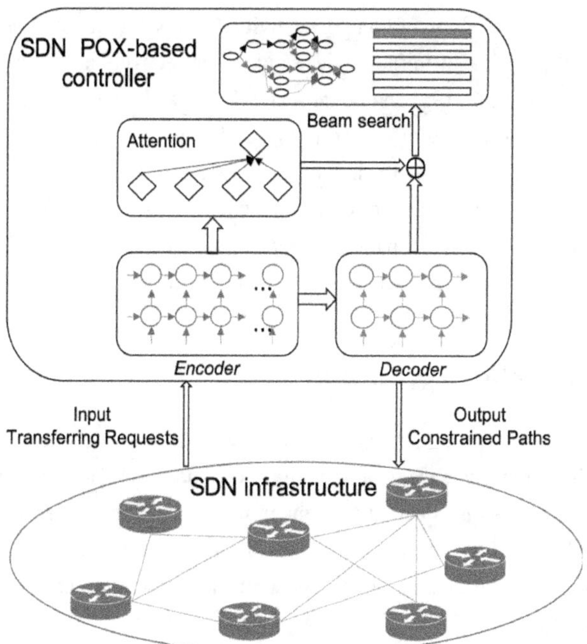

Fig. 5.1 A High-level Illustration of The Proposed Forwarding Method Based on Seq2Seq Model

For simplicity, Eqs. (1) and (2) can be re-written as follows:

$$y_i^j = \mathscr{F}(\overrightarrow{\mathbf{y}_i^{-j}}, \theta, \omega | \overrightarrow{\mathbf{x}_i}), \quad \overrightarrow{\mathbf{x}_i} \in \mathscr{D}_s, \quad \overrightarrow{\mathbf{y}_i} \in \mathscr{D}_t,$$
$$i = 1, 2, 3, ..., k, \quad j = 1, 2, 3, ..., n_y \tag{5.3}$$

Normally, $\overrightarrow{\mathbf{x}_i}$ is a two-element sequence, source x_{src} and destination x_{dst} for basic for-warding. Meanwhile, with a constrained condition, $\overrightarrow{\mathbf{x}_i}$ will include particular network nodes, e.g. node IDs, through which a flow should go. This can be expressed as:

$$y_i^j = \mathscr{F}(\overrightarrow{\mathbf{y}_i^{-j}}, \theta, \omega | x_{src}, x_{res}, x_{dst}),$$
$$x_{src}, x_{res}, x_{dst} \in \mathscr{D}_s, \quad \overrightarrow{\mathbf{y}_i} \in \mathscr{D}_t,$$
$$i = 1, 2, 3, ..., k, \quad j = 1, 2, 3, ..., n_y \tag{5.4}$$

It is worth noting that x_{res} represents a single restricted node, whereas a set of restricted nodes can be added, namely, $\overrightarrow{x_{res}} = \{x_{res1}, x_{res2}, ...\} \subset \mathscr{D}_s$.

Because the sequence output from standard seq2seq model could be variant in statistics due to flexibility and randomness, the network path represented by the target sequence,

y_i^j, may encounter the problem of non-connectivity. This is not tolerant in the forwarding method for path planning in traffic engineering. To effectively alleviate this issue, the attention mechanism [102, 191] and beam search [192] will be employed. The attention mechanism is an enhancement for context relevancy learning, and the beam search tops the best score and attempts to ensure the link connectivity. The details of leveraging attention mechanism and beam search can be found in Sections 5.3.4 and 5.3.5. The situation of rarely happened non-connectivity path in the target sequence after the adoption of attention mechanism and beam search is discussed at the end of Section 5.3.5.

5.3 Background Techniques

The seq2seq model [190] is an expanded and specific encoder-decoder model in neural networks for handling sequence data, including sequence data learning, transferring and translation. It now prevails in neural machine translation, text summarization and speech recognition in Natural Language Processing (NLP), image captioning and other sequence data applications. In this section, an overview of the formulation and the details of the seq2seq model is given.

5.3.1 Recurrent neural network

In this section, the Recurrent Neural Network (RNN) is introduced, which is particularly devised for sequential modeling in neural networks. RNN has gained its popularity and shown promising performance thanks to its capability of taking information from past to subsequent inputs.

In detail, RNN attempts to *memorize* sequential histories and merge them into current observation in order to predict the next sample element in the same sequence. The *"memory"* unit is usually called *cell*. A simple architecture of RNN is presented in Fig. 5.2.

In Fig. 5.2, it can be seen that at time step t, an input sample x_t is pushed into a cell, based on which the hidden state s_t is generated. Ultimately, the output o_t would be given by the hidden state s_t.

The hidden states and outputs can be represented in a mathematical way as follows:

- $s_t = f(Ux_t + Ws_{t-1})$, where U is an input matrix and W is the weights;

- $o_t = softmax(Vs_t)$, where V is an output matrix mapping the hidden state s_t into classification scores;

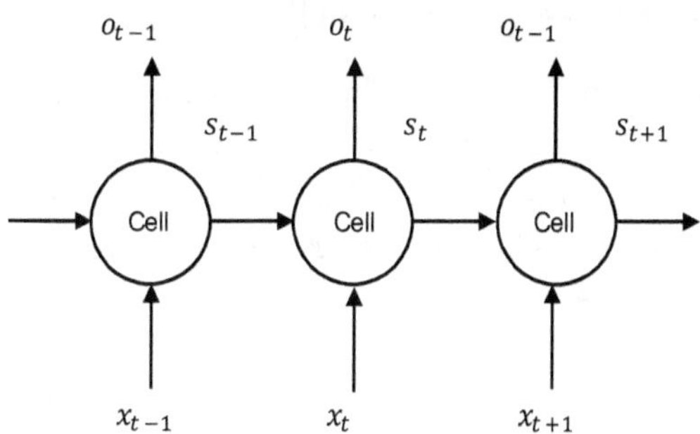

Fig. 5.2 A Simple Architecture of RNN.

- $f(\cdot)$ is considered as the core component, widely accepted as the basic cell $tanh(\cdot)$, Long Short Term Memory (LSTM) cell [193] and Gated Recurrent Unit (GRU) cell [194].

5.3.2 The Encoder-Decoder structure

The goal of Encoder-Decoder structure is regarded as a mechanism to map the data in the source space into the desired information in the target space via an intermedia space. Specifically, two parts are included: *Encoder* and *Decoder*. Let x and y denote the data in the source space and target space, respectively, and m represent the data in the intermedia space. Therefore, it has

$$Encoder: \overrightarrow{m} = En(\overrightarrow{x}), \forall \overrightarrow{x} \in D_s, \forall \overrightarrow{m} \in D_m$$

$$Decoder: \overrightarrow{y} = De(\overrightarrow{m}), \forall \overrightarrow{y} \in D_t, \forall \overrightarrow{m} \in D_m$$

where D_s is the source space with dimension l_x, D_m is the intermediate space with dimension l_m, and D_t is the target space with dimension l_y.

The Encoder-Decoder structure is able to learn the source space knowledge to align with the desired target space knowledge, referred as "*translation*" or "*transduction*" in some cases.

Note that the setting of $D_s = D_t$ ensures that the constrained path planning problem in traffic engineering, considering the request pairs (source -> destination nodes) and the constrained conditions (source -> constraints -> destination), can be fitted into this scheme, because they are in the same objective space as controlled network nodes.

5.3.3 The sequence-to-sequence model

The seq2seq model was proposed in [190] for neural machine translation, which now is extended as general-purpose sequential model in many other spheres, for instance, conversational modeling, image captioning, etc. An evident advantage of seq2seq model is that it can encode variable length sequences into a fixed-length coding vector bridging the gap between source space and target space.

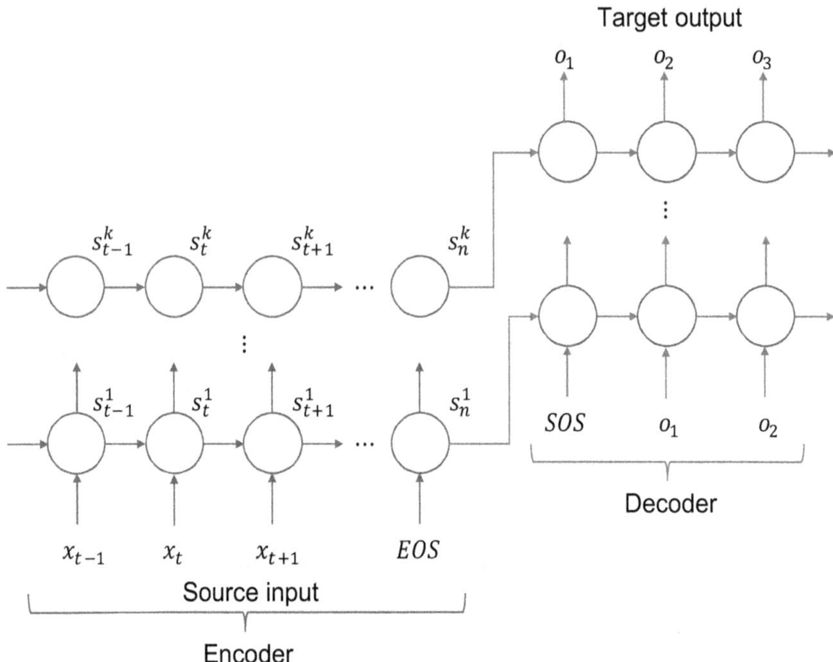

Fig. 5.3 An Abstract Structure of Seq2Seq Model.

A illustration of the seq2seq model is depicted in Fig. 5.3. As can be seen, two parts are included: *Encoder* marked red and *Decoder* marked blue. With the source input $\vec{x}$, adding an ending symbol, EOS, there can be stacked by multiple layers of the RNN instances in *Encoder* compressing ordered information into final hidden states, which is then sent to the counterparts in *Decoder*. On the opposite side, *Decoder* takes the hidden states and the estimated outputs, adding a starting symbol, SOS, as the initialization and inputs of its corresponding RNN instances, respectively.

5.3.4   Attention mechanism

The attention mechanism, also named alignment, has been applied in [102, 191], aiming at aligning the elements of a sentence or a phrase in a correct order in neural machine translation. In this study, it is adapted to ensure reasonable sequence order by scoring the relevance of the elements between source space and target space.

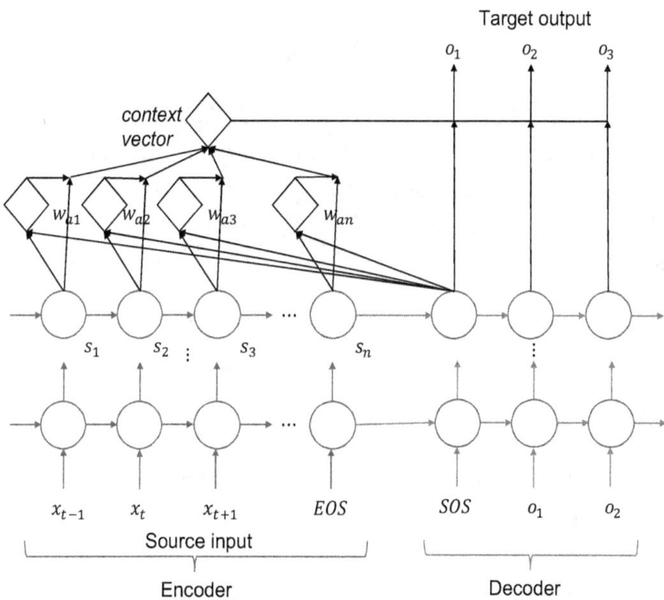

Fig. 5.4 An Illustration of Attention Mechanism

Fig. 5.4 illustrates the basic idea of attention mechanism. Instead of directly using encoder hidden states, the attention mechanism sums up the encoder hidden states as the context vector by weights w_{ai}, which are scored with decoder hidden states. Thus, along with the context vector, the model also takes hidden states of the last decoder layer as comprehensive information to obtain the final target outputs. The score function could be multiplicative or additive, depicted in [102, 191].

Because the attention mechanism captures key relevance, we take advantage of it to effectively restore the complete restricted forwarding paths. The *Decoder* can therefore use the context vector $\overrightarrow{c}$ with the last decoding hidden state $\overrightarrow{\mathbf{h}_D}$ as follows:

$$\varphi_i = \mathscr{F}_{Attention}(h_{E,i}, h_{D,t-1})$$

$$\forall i, 1 \leq i \leq n_x \tag{5.5}$$

$$\forall t, 1 \leq t \leq n_y$$

$$\alpha_i = softmax(\varphi_i) \tag{5.6}$$

$$\overrightarrow{c_t} = \sum_i \alpha_i \cdot h_{E,i} \tag{5.7}$$

where the relevance score between *Encoder* hidden states $h_{E,i}, 1 \leq i \leq n_x$ and the *Decoder* previous step hidden state $h_{D,t-1}$ is denoted as φ_i. α_i is the weight for *Encoder* hidden states to compute weighted sum of the context vector, $\overrightarrow{c_t}$.

The final output of target sequence with the context vectors taken into account can be expressed as:

$$y_i^j = \mathscr{F}(\overrightarrow{\mathbf{y}_i^{-j}}, \theta, \omega, \overrightarrow{c_i} \,|\, \overrightarrow{\mathbf{x}_i}) \tag{5.8}$$

$$y_i^j = \mathscr{F}(\overrightarrow{\mathbf{y}_i^{-j}}, \theta, \omega, \overrightarrow{c_i} \,|\, x_{src}, x_{res}, x_{dst}) \tag{5.9}$$

where Eq. (5.8) shows the output without constrained condition, and Eq. (5.9) denotes that with constrained condition taken into account.

5.3.5 Beam search

The aforementioned LSTM cell, the seq2seq structure and the attention mechanism enormously facilitate sequential data sensing and cognition. However, the single output result (i.e., only one target output) may cause local optimum. Especially, sequential models normally cannot rerun, failing to circumvent temporary single highest score and gain rewards in the long run. A potential solution is to collect as many candidate traces as possible to avoid this local optimum problem. Hence, in this study the beam search algorithm [192] is adapted to achieve this purpose and boost the performance of the proposed model.

The idea of beam search is to widen the model search range by buffering n traces, which provides a list of outputs by scoring the sequence context. n is the beam search width. A simple example is presented in Fig. 5.5, where 7 paths are drawn with 7 colors, marked with starting symbol, SOS, and ending symbol, EOS. Beam search can efficiently explore the target space and output the top-n paths against the single result. Compared to breadth search,

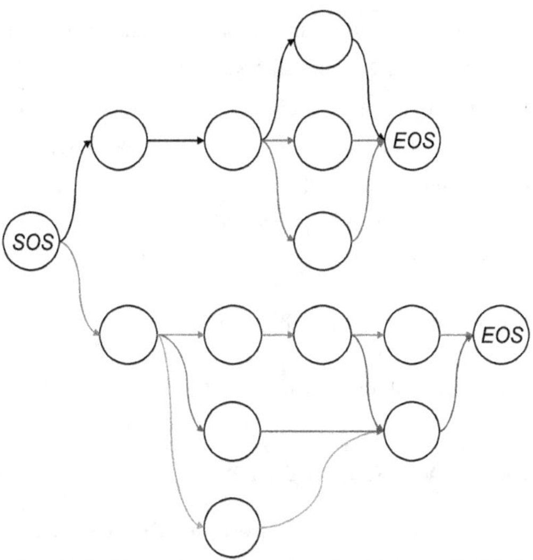

Fig. 5.5 An Example of Beam Search with Beam Width-7

which exhausts all options, beam search eliminates highly unlikely traces to accelerates training and testing.

In this study, beam search is adapted in the *Decoder* not only for providing optimal target output, but also for presenting the target output as valid forwarding path. Let beam search width n be 5, a list of top 5 sequences are therefore buffered. From the top 1 to the last (i.e., 5 in this case), any duplicate nodes are eliminated canceling wasteful loops, and checking whether the successor node is a neighbor of the previous node to verify the connectivity of forwarding path of the output target.

It is worth noting that the consideration of attention mechanism and beam search can still miss a very small fraction of path validity (path non-connectivity) from the empirical results. As a matter of the fact, it can conduct the last guarantee via recomputing the non-connectivity path. For example, if all 5 candidates lose their validity, it chooses the top 1 and recomputes the path between the disconnected node and the destination. In practice, this situation may lead to long delay, however it occurs very rarely.

5.4   Experiments and Analysis

In this section, experiments are conducted to evaluate the effectiveness of the proposed learning-based path planning model under constrained conditions. SDN is used as the network environment due to its popularity and pervasive application in traffic engineering

[8]. In this section, it employs the Mininet emulator [195], and deploy the proposed learning-based forwarding model in POX, a typical and popular implementation of SDN controller, to make decisions for path planning under constrained conditions. Mininet emulates a virtual network with a set of virtual hosts that can run various network services. It is specifically designed for SDN scenario embedded with OpenFlow specification.

In what follows, the environment settings will be shown, as well as the results and discussions. The experiments consist of two major parts:

1. The training and evaluation of seq2seq model

2. SDN network simulation employing the model

5.4.1 The seq2seq model training process

The seq2seq model is built on top of the TensorFlow library published by Google [196]. Two types of network topology are selected in the evaluation: the 2012 Europe GEANT network topology with 40 nodes, shown in Fig. 5.6, and a 10x10 Grid network topology with 100 nodes, shown in Fig. 5.7. The Europe GEANT is a widely used network backbone infrastructure which provides high broad-band and high quality services for academic connections. The GEANT as well as the standard grid topology shows typical network structures and the traffic on both two topologies may reflect complex and practical traffic patterns. The bandwidth is also constrained between switches [1] as 50Mbps and link delay as 2ms. Meanwhile, to eliminate the impact of connection between host and switch on network performance, the host-switch link bandwidth is set to be 1000Mbps with 2ms link delay. In the experiments, it sets the constrained condition, $\overrightarrow{x_{res}}$, to be one-node and multi-node (i.e., two nodes), respectively. Namely, the planned network path between source and destination need go through one particular node (one node constrained) and two particular nodes (multi-node constrained) in the network. In the following, we will show training data preparation and the training and evaluating of the proposed model, for each of the two topologies.

- **Training data preparation**

To collect the training data, we first implement the Dijkstra's shortest path algorithm to generate a collection of static paths between nodes in a network. The shortest paths between nodes are usually not unique, but the focus is on the unicast scheme and extract only one for each source and destination pair. These paths are considered as empirical effective paths. In

---

[1] In SDN, network nodes are called switches.

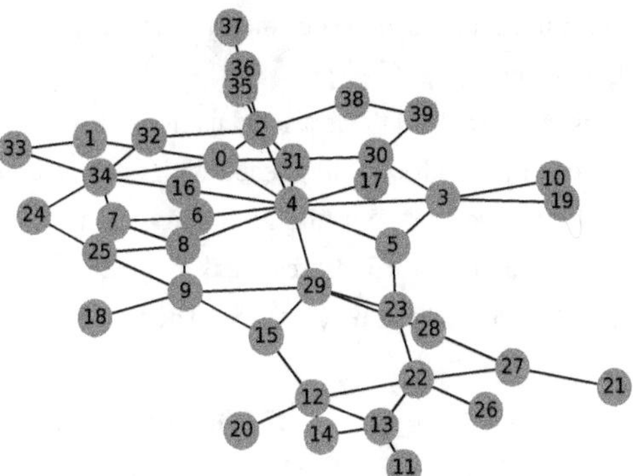

Fig. 5.6 The Topology of Europe GEANT Network

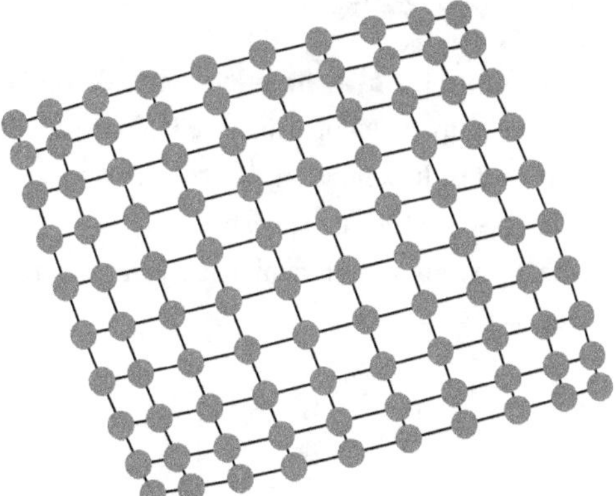

Fig. 5.7 The Topology of 10x10 Grid Network

addition to these empirical effective paths, it shall generate the *restricted experiences* as the experiences for traffic forwarding under constrained conditions.

First of all, the data preparation for one-node constraint (i.e., the path between source and destination need go through a given node) is detailed below, followed by the multi-node constraint (for the convenience of presentation, two-node constraint is considered).

To obtain the restricted experiences, all network nodes will get chance to be selected as the restricted node (one is selected each time) except for the ones that have already been in the paths collected for empirical effective paths and those that lead to routing loops (the examples will be provided below to illustrate this routing loop situation). In order to form the *restricted paths* (the paths collected for restricted experiences) with the one-node constraint, two separated paths are calculated: the one between the source and the constrained node and the one between the constrained node and the destination, respectively. Then, these two paths are concatenated as the restricted path.

The example below is how to collect the restricted paths in the GEANT network topology. It considers two scenarios of traffic forwarding, each with one constrained node. The first scenario has node 1 as the source, node 5 as the destination, and node 2 as the constrained node, i.e., $x_{src} = 1$, $x_{res} = 2$, and $x_{dst} = 5$, represented by $(1,2,5)$. A second scenario has $x_{src} = 1$, $x_{res} = 16$, and $x_{dst} = 5$, denoted by $(1,16,5)$. The two separated paths for $(1,2,5)$ are:

$$(1,2) \Rightarrow (1,0,2), \quad (2,5) \Rightarrow (2,0,4,5),$$

and the two separated paths for $(1,16,5)$ are:

$$(1,16) \Rightarrow (1,33,34,16), \quad (16,5) \Rightarrow (16,4,5).$$

The path for the scenario of $(1,2,5)$ will not be collected as the restricted path for restricted experiences, because a routing loop is involved in this path due to the overlapped node 0 in these two separate paths. In contrast, the path for the scenario of $(1,16,5)$ will be collected as the restricted path for restricted experiences.

One sample data in the dataset for model training is a pair of source and destination and the path for the target sequence:

$$\{(1,5),(1,0,4,5)\},$$

or

$$\{(1,16),(1,33,34,16)\}.$$

When generating the restricted paths for restricted experiences, the method also considers the number of hops in the network, i.e., only collecting the paths whose length in terms of hops between source and destination is equal to or less than 20. Table 5.1 shows the size of collected data based on the length of paths. Note that there is no big difference between the data size when considering different path lengths in GEANT network topology. That is because most of the forwarding paths between any random source and destination pair are close to 10 hops. Therefore, in the experiments, it trains and tests the proposed model using GEANT network topology with the path length of 20, as it contains the cases of path length of 10 and 15 hops.

Table 5.2 presents the data size for training and testing dataset split by the ratio of 80%:20%. Note, as mentioned above, only the path length of 20 in GEANT network is used for training.

Table 5.1 Data Size By Path Length of One-node Constrain

	Length = 10	Length = 15	Length = 20
GEANT	16094	17946	17962
Grid	89086	290424	421844

Table 5.2 Data Size of The Training and Testing Set of One-node Constrain

		Length = 10	Length = 15	Length = 20
GEANT	Training			14369
	Testing			3593
Grid	Training	71269	232339	337475
	testing	17817	58085	84369

On top of one-node constraint dataset, two-node constraint dataset is easily constructed and the path representation is very similar. Firstly a source and destination pair is selected as the objective, then search the extracted one-node constraint dataset to pick all paths that share the same source but are not embedded into its shortest path. Finally, it concatenates the one-node constrained path with the destination as the two-node constrained path. An example is presented below:

Suppose the pair $(1,3)$ to be a two-node constrained path. In one-node constrained path dataset, it has the path of $(1,16,5)$ as $(1,33,34,16,4,5)$. It is easy to check that $(1,16,5)$ is not a segment of the shortest path of $(1,3)$. As such, $(1,16,5,3)$ shall be the two-node constrained path of the pair $(1,3)$,

$$(1,16,5) \Rightarrow (1,33,34,16,4,5), \quad (5,3) \Rightarrow (5,3)$$

and the complete path shall be:

$$(1,16,5,3) \Rightarrow (1,33,34,16,4,5,3)$$

The dataset size is shown in Table 5.5.

- **Training and evaluating the proposed model**

As has been described in the above sections, setting of the hyper-parameters of the proposed model is as follows: in the *Encoder*, two stacked bi-directional LSTM layers are adopted, which can be regarded as four layers. As opposite, the *Decoder* has four uni-directional LSTM layers. The size of hidden layer is 1024, the embedding size is 100 for nodes (e.g., their IDs) mapping into a vector space, and the beam search width is 5. The model is trained using the mini-batch method with batch size 100 and the Adam optimizer [197]. The experiments are run in a server with Intel 24-core Xeon E5-2650 CPU, 32GB memory and GTX GeForce 1080Ti. The training results of GEANT network topology and grid network topology are shown in Table 5.3 and Table 5.4, respectively.

Table 5.3 The Accuracy of The Training and Evaluating of The Proposed Model in The GEANT Network

		Beam=1 Length=20	Beam=5 Length=20
GEANT	Training	0.9794	1.0
	Testing	0.9740	0.9991

Table 5.4 The Accuracy of The Training and Evaluating of The Proposed Model in The Grid Network

		Beam=5		
		Length=10	Length=15	Length=20
Grid	Training	1.0	0.9990	0.9998
	Testing	0.9901	0.9984	0.9987

Table 5.3 indicates that beam search helps gain better performance of the model. The beam width of 1 refers to the situation that only the first outcome is taken into consideration, while beam width of 5 refers to the situation that the model will output 5 candidate paths, and if there is any disconnected path found, the model will move to the next candidate and perform the same check.

An intriguing discovery of path inference is worth to note. Since the dataset contains non-restricted paths (shortest paths in this study) and restricted paths, and it is evenly randomly split into training and testing set, the model might not witness the shortest path, i.e., $\{(1,5),(1,0,4,5)\}$ may only occur in testing data. The model is somehow still able to discover the corresponding non-restricted path. That is $\{(1,5),(1,0,4,5)\}$ is not witnessed in training, nevertheless the model can still output $(1,0,4,5)$ with the input $(1,5)$. The conjecture is that the neural network is capable of extracting sub-sequential structure embedded in a super-sequence. This feature implies that the proposed model can effectively capture correct paths with partial experiences. Another fact is there is still a tiny fraction of paths that cannot be covered to guarantee their connectivity. A final check will be conduct to fix this problem.

Furthermore, the experiments are extended to two-node constraint as an example of multi-node constraint, where the collection is based on one-node constraint, as described above.

Table 5.5 The Accuracy of The Training and Testing in Two-node Constraint Experiments and Dataset Size, Beam Width=5.

	Training	Testing	Data Size
GEANT	1.0	0.9999	154663
Grid	0.9993	0.9999	4038738

Table 5.5 shows the accuracy of the training and testing with two-node constraint experiments. The data sizes of two network collections, GEANT and Grid topology, are 154663 and 4038738, respectively.

5.4.2 SDN emulation experiments with learning-based controller

In what follows, we will introduce the details of the experiment results conducted by the proposed model. In order to show the performance of the proposed model, it uses the result from the model for the network without any constrained conditions as the baseline. The results of one-node constraint are shown in Table 5.6 and Table 5.7, respectively, for GEANT topology and grid topology. The throughput and delay are of interests to present how much influence the constrain condition will impose on actual traffic. The delay is the actual transferring delay without traffic congestion and the congestion delay directly refers to transferring delay under traffic congestion.

Each switch is binded with a host to generate packets. 100 source-destination pairs are randomly selected. Clearly, the 100 pairs interfere with each other heavily, which causes frequent request conflicts and bandwidth competition. Hence, the network congestion happens frequently as well.

Table 5.6 Experiment Results of One-node Constraint in The GEANT Network

		Throughput	Congest Delay	Delay
Non-res		1136.15Mbps	295.45ms	15.62ms
Res	100%	711.48Mbps	343.36ms	23.21ms
	50%	908.04Mbps	312.49ms	20.02ms
	20%	1048.17Mbps	307.03ms	16.74ms

Table 5.7 Experiment Results of One-node Constraint in The Grid Network

		Throughput	Congest Delay	Delay
Non-res		1267.67Mbps	329.13ms	25.71ms
Res	100%	781.39Mbps	344.29ms	41.15ms
	50%	1105.09Mbps	380.40ms	33.00ms
	20%	1217.33Mbps	364.47ms	36.76ms

In Table 5.6 and Table 5.7, three metrics of network performance are presented, i.e., average throughput, delay in congested condition, and delay in non-congested condition. "Non-res" represents the network without any constrained conditions, and "Res" denotes the network with constrained conditions. The percentage in "Res" indicates the volume of traffic that are forwarded by restricted paths. Note that, as the main work is focusing on proposing a learning-based forwarding strategy, at this point, the forwarding strategy is to randomly choose a constrained node without taking the performance metrics into account. It is reasonable that the random pick might deteriorate the throughput because the paths may lead to unexpectedly long path. It therefore overlaps with more other traffic paths, which triggers more traffic congestion.

As can be seen from the results shown in Table 5.6 and Table 5.7, despite the performance being polluted under 100% restricted paths, it is not affected heavily for regulating a part of traffic in both topologies. 20% restrictions show very promising throughput since it is very close to baseline result (network performance under no constrained conditions). As for delay of the network with constrained conditions, both congested and non-congested conditions have no big difference compared with the network without any constrained conditions, emphasizing the superiority of the proposed model.

For two-node constraint experiment results, in Table 5.8 and Table 5.9, three experiments are conducted, measured by three performance metrics.

Table 5.8 Experiment Results of Two-node Constraint in The GEANT Network

		Throughput	Congestion Delay	Delay
Non-res		1136.15Mbps	295.45ms	15.62ms
Res	100%	494.32Mbps	373.97ms	29.08ms
	50%	877.31Mbps	358.21ms	22.27ms
	20%	1076.22Mbps	338.40ms	18.24ms

For GEANT topology, the throughput of 100% one-node constraint paths is significantly higher than that of two-node constraint paths as well as the counterpart of grid topology.

Table 5.9 Experiment Results of Two-node Constraint in The Grid Network

		Throughput	Congestion Delay	Delay
Non-res		1267.67Mbps	329.13ms	25.71ms
Res	100%	690.67Mbps	378.26ms	40.01ms
	50%	1056.25Mbps	358.82ms	31.67ms
	20%	1242.23Mbps	390.22ms	28.79ms

However, in 50% situation, the throughput of two-node constraint are just slightly below the one-node case, in both two network topologies. It is worth noting that the throughput of two-node constraint is slightly higher than that of one-node situation. This may indicate that the network transferring with more hops do not always cause more interference. It conjectures that some of two-node constraint paths truly circumvent local busy cliques, which trades off delay but reduces routing conflicts. It also brings the chance that reasonable paths planning could increase the network throughput trading off acceptable delays to achieve optimized network utility.

There are numerous case studies that require fine-grained traffic engineering, e.g., traffic filtering, load balancing, and firewall. The work leverages the experiences learned from historical traffic data, which abundantly exist in current Internet, to achieve this target. The self-learning feature of the proposed model intends to make full use of existing experiences to discover implicit traffic trend.

5.5 Summary

In this chapter, it proposes a learning-based network-level forwarding method for path planning in the network with constrained conditions. It has sought to introduce well-defined deep learning model into network traffic engineering sphere by formulating the traffic forwarding problem as a sequence prediction problem. The learning-based model has been developed for traffic forwarding based on the sequence-to-sequence model enhanced by attention mechanism and beam search. The proposed model has been implemented in the controller of an SDN architecture in Mininet emulator. Experiment results have shown the superiority of the proposed model in path planning in the network with constrained conditions.

Chapter 6

Dynamic Network Traffic Engineering: A Reinforcement Learning Perspective

6.1   Introduction

The network traffic engineering optimization issues have been discussed in Chapter. 5 with supervised-based sequence to sequence model. The learnable model makes the most of the hidden values in history data and effectively generalizes to unseen situations to obtain optimal or approximately optimal outcomes. The supervised paradigm is able to offer a straightforward idea for most of work to converge to the stable and consistent performance, which has been well studied for decades.

Admittedly, the supervised algorithms facilitate intelligent decision agents to execute optimal instructions, the supervised learning is solely applicable to well prepared and labeled data for learning process convergence. The labeled data require massive and costly manual workload, which almost prevents broader applications and sharply reduces the efficiency of problem solving. Another drawback is the disparity between the obsolete model and unexpected future data distributions. The pre-defined learnable model seeks to discovery implicit pattern from history data and apply the possibly stale knowledge to the future situations, which ignores feasible changes of dynamically generated data. As such, in this chapter, the main focus is a reasonable scheme to fit the dynamics and avoid the influence of expensive manually labeled work. Network resource optimization and traffic engineering dose not only benefit from knowledge learning and insight, but also strongly involves in making decision and taking actions. Hence, a dynamic decision making process provides a clear approach to accommodate this problem.

The real network environment is unstable and dynamic for the complex architecture and fluctuating service demands, changing the optimal conditions constantly. The unstable environment brings about ever-changing data patterns and requires relatively complicated models to fit data, which even aggravates the burden of analysis and decision-making. The Reinforcement Learning (RL) [198] copes with the optimal and long-term decision-making problems in a dynamic environment and has a decent property to match the traffic engineering scope. Recently, the RL, strengthened by Deep Learning (DL) advances, has reached the beyond-expert level [132, 199, 200] in different games, showing promising and impressive performance in dynamic applications. The combination between RL and DL refers to the phrase of Deep Reinforcement Learning (DRL), and it gains popularities and reputations in Artificial Intelligence.

6.2 Preliminaries

Different from the traditional supervised learning and unsupervised learning algorithms, the Reinforcement learning attempts to accommodate constantly changing scenarios to find the largest performance earning in a long term with respect to specific problem settings.

6.2.1 Overview of Reinforcement Learning

Fig. 6.1 illustrates the fundamental process of general Reinforcement Learning with two basic blocks, the intelligent agent and the object environment, respectively, where $0 < i < \infty$. The main assumption of Reinforcement Learning is Markov Decision Process (MDP) [201]. When starting at an initial state, the agent makes decision to take an action a_i in effect in the object environment. Then environment receives the information and its state has been changed, resulting in a reward r_i. The state has been changed to another one and exposes an observation, o_i, for the agent to identify. It is worthy to note that the real state is likely to represent the state as s_i at i step while in Fig. 6.1, there is an observation, o_i. In effect, the target environments are highly complicated with enormous correlated components, which makes the true states very vague and abundant. Practically, the true implicit states are difficult to be fully recognized except partial but highly relevant information. In this regard, the observation o_i is presented as a reference of the partial state.

Theoretically, the MDP is also a stochastic process but in discrete time with elastic decisions (action taking). From the perspective of human, it is a normal demand to obtain an optimal (maximizing benefits or minimizing damages) performance in terms of particular measures interacting with different environments. The environments always fail to remain

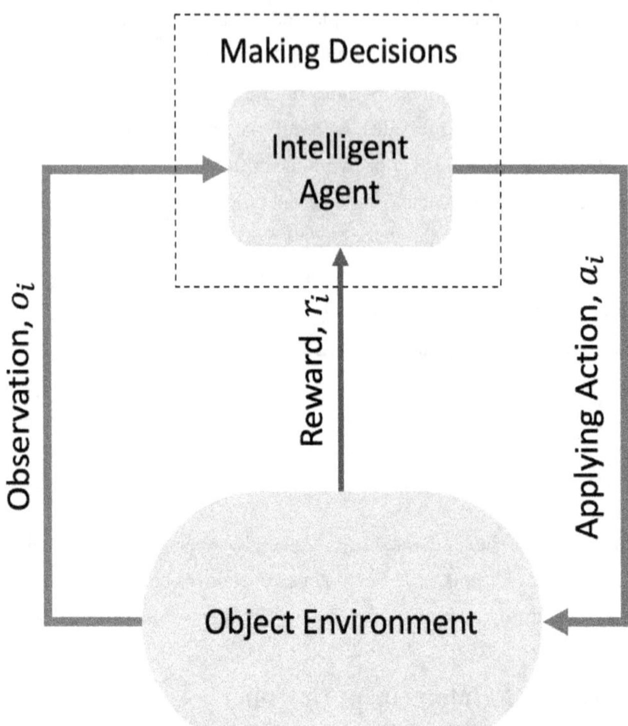

Fig. 6.1 Classic Reinforcement Learning Process in A Feedback Loop

similar so that the design of optimal solutions deeply depends on the unsteady background situation and the underlying states. The underlying states are time-varying and the ideal solution has an elastic strategy to determine what behavior should appear in terms of long run benefits. Assume that the changing of underlying states is a Markov chain where the next step state solely depends on the current and the changing cause is from outside force (action taking). When one action is taken based on the current state and the current state consequently changes to another, an immediate feedback (reward) will be given to tell how well it does at the time slot. Then the entire process with feedbacks can be called Markov Decision Process. The entire is from observing the environment and inferring hidden states to receiving a reward once apply an action into the environment. Thus an intelligent agent should be involved in finding a strategy by the state analysis to guarantee the long term earning is the optimal.

The MDP can be modeled as a tuple of (S, A, P, R), depicted in the following:

- S denotes a set of environment states;

- A denotes a set of operational actions applied to environment;

- P denotes dynamic state transition probability; in particular, $P_a(s_t, s_{t+1})$ represents the transition probability from state s_t to s_{t+1} when taking action a, where $a \in A$, and $s_t, s_{t+1} \in S$;

- R denotes an immediate reward; in particular, $R_a(s_t, s_{t+1})$ is the received reward if the state transition s_t to s_{t+1} occurs when taking action a.

As aforementioned, the state S is highly likely to be latent due to the complexity and heterogeneity of the network system. The observation O as the partial state, solely represents the necessary part and may vary based on specific tasks. Here, t denotes the time step, $0 < t < \infty$. In practice, the state will terminate until a terminal condition is reached.

The core object of reinforcement learning is to maximize a series of accumulated rewards along with consecutive actions for one task. The accumulated rewards is the total value, V, of interest, sometimes also called the total return.

$$V_0 = \gamma_0 R_0 + \gamma_1 R_1 + ... + \gamma_t R_t + ..., t \rightarrow \infty$$
$$= \sum_{i=0}^{\infty} \gamma_i R_i, \gamma_0 = 1 \tag{6.1}$$

V_0 is the accumulated values at time 0 based on a set of consecutive actions $a_0, a_1, ..., a_t$. Here, γ refers to a discount factor to control the influence from actions at every time point. R_i is the corresponding reward. The action a_i is selected by the policy $a_i = \pi_i(s_i)$ on top of the state s_i. When there exists a policy, π_M, making the value the maximal, the policy $\pi_M = \pi^*$ is called the optimal policy.

Apparently, the policy is of special interest, since the value heavily depends on it and the intelligent agent will practically realize it to take effective actions to gain the largest benefit. At the beginning, the adopted policy is likely to be random so that the entire process is to iteratively update the policy and ultimately reach the convergence. In general, there are two main branches, value-based policy optimization [202] and immediate policy gradient optimization [84, 203]. Based on the two ideas, recent researches have gained a vast amount of remarkable successes [204–209].

It has drawn many attentions to both researchers and pragmatics and achieved decent performance in numerous applications, such as computing resource management [210], city traffic control [211], robotics [212], and games [132, 199, 200] even over human rivals. Especially in networking traffic engineering, recently advances [10, 11] bridge the gap between highly variant and dynamic traffic engineering and sampling-inefficient decision-making methods. In the section below, an technical overview of the well-known Q-learning is introduced, which is adopted to deal with dynamic traffic issues.

6.2.2 Deep Q-learning

As for Deep Q-learning, there can be viewed as two divisions, Q-learning fundamentals [202] and Deep learning-enhanced. Q-learning refers to a model-free value-based algorithm as a classic approach of Reinforcement Learning. Here, the model-free is an idea that the solution takes on account of state transition probability $P_a(s_t, s_{t+1})$ but makes the most of estimated total values with a specific action. In contrast to model-free, the model-based idea leverages the state transition dynamics to guide the learning part in the correct direction. Note that the term "*model*" in both model-free and model-based is for the transition dynamics probability, not as the same as general deep learning model.

More detailed, Q-learning emphasizes the action should be taken considering the current state and the subsequent results following the current optimal strategy. In essence, the convergence belongs to the value-iteration update process. From Eq. 6.1, it can be easily reformed as iteration-based update in Eq. 6.2, where $V^{(i)}$ is the value of i-th iteration over the current strategy π. Here, $0 < i < \infty$. This formation is also referred as Bellman Equation [198]. For the very first iteration, $i = 0$, $V^{(1)}$ is obtained by the $V^{(0)}$, which is initialized as a fixed guess, such as 0. With the iteration progressing, the value is inclined to converge and the strategy is taken as actions triggering the optimal values. The strategy π_{s_i} is formulated in Eq. 6.3.

$$V_\pi^{(i+1)}(s_i) = \sum_{s_i} P(s_i, s_{i+1})(R(s_i, s_{i+1}) + \gamma V_\pi^{(i)}(s_{i+1})) \tag{6.2}$$

$$\pi_{s_i} = \arg\max_a V(s_i) = \arg\max_a \sum_{s_i} P(s_i, s_{i+1})(R(s_i, s_{i+1}) + \gamma V(s_{i+1})) \tag{6.3}$$

Q-learning inherits the above value iteration process and obtains the strategy based on Eq. 6.3 as well. Nevertheless, the Q-learning achieves better convergence speed by substituting the state value expression, V with action-value expression, Q, which explicitly emphasizes the consequence of a specific action in a state, followed by the strategy π rather than the expected value over all possible actions. Eq. 6.4 formulates the Q-value function employed in Q-learning, which highlights the adopted action a. The difference between Eq. 6.2 and Eq. 6.4. is that the value iteration is the expected value over the policy probability distribution while the Q function focuses on one specific action.

$$Q(s,a) = \sum_{s_i} P(s_i, s_{i+1}; a)(R(s_i, s_{i+1}; a) + \gamma V^{(i)}(s_{i+1})) \tag{6.4}$$

In general, the Q-learning algorithm works well in size-limited scenarios, where states are finite and traversable. The limited size state space is then modeled as a tabular paradigm and the state transition can be determined by a look-up table. However, the state size in most real cases is always so large that the tabular mode works extremely inefficiently, even totally fails in the continuous state space with infinite states. A suitable estimator for the finite state space is in an urgent need for pragmatic problems.

In effect, there are numerous methods to approximate the Q function [198], such as linear approximator and deep neural networks. Hence the second division *"Deep"* is introduced to construct the Deep Q-learning. The Deep Learning fundamentals include various building blocks, e.g., fully connected network, and Long Short Term Memory. Sometimes, the fully connected network refers to artificial neural network. It can consist of versatile linear or non-linear function as the activation function, for instance, Sigmoid, Hyperbolic Tangent and the Relu function. Empirically, the fully connected network is a preferable option for non-sequential discrete data with a linear function at the last one-node output layer. The model takes as input the combination of the environment state representation and the taken action to ultimately transform into a single value output as the state-action Q-value. The Q-value update conforms to the iteration mechanism of state-value V function, and finally the strategy is approximately created based on Eq. 6.3.

6.3   Problem Formulation

Definition 5.2.1 gives a clear definition for path planning and learning between source and destination nodes. Under such definition, Chapter 5 dedicates to supervised learning model constrained by conditions. Nonetheless the labeled target paths merely conform to the stale network configurations and settings rather than offering agile and flexible solutions for an unstable and dynamic surrounding. In this section, the object converts from a static and fixed issue to a dynamic and flexible problem. There are two types of core work: one is inspired from Chapter 5, finding an intermediate constrained node to maximize constrained path throughput, and the other is the construction of the complete sequence.

The optimization in the constrain condition: in Chapter 5, the evaluation of the constrain condition is randomly selecting the constrained forwarding node. Here, in order to minimize the throughput loss of the constrained scheme, the intelligent agent attempts to search the optimal constrained node based on the current network state to improve throughput.

The formulation conforms to the definition in Chapter 5. In this section, the optimization is only for the one-node condition.

The optimization in the dynamic forwarding path planning: we assume a data transferring plane in SDN network is abstracted as a graph topology, G. Let V and E be the respective vertex set and the edge set of graph G, where $|V| = \phi_v$ and $|E| = \phi_e$. The number of vertex in V is ϕ_v and the number of edge in E is ϕ_e. Provided that the $< \xi_s, \xi_d >$ is a pair of traffic source node and destination node, $\xi_s \neq \xi_d, \xi_s, \xi_d \in V$, and a source sequence $s_{seq} = (\xi_s, \xi_1, \xi_2, ... \xi_{mid})$, where $\xi_i \neq \xi_j$ if $i \neq j$, $\xi_i \in V$, $(\xi_i, \xi_{i+1}) \in E$, the object is to find a target sequence $t_{seq} = (\xi_{mid}, \xi_1', \xi_2', ..., \xi_d')$, where $\xi_i' \neq \xi_j'$ if $i \neq j$, $\xi_i' \in V$, $(\xi_i', \xi_{i+1}') \in E$, so that $s_{seq} \cap t_{seq} = \xi_{mid}$. Then the union of two sets, s_{seq} and t_{seq} as $s_{seq} \cup t_{seq}$, is a complete path from the source node, ξ_s, to the destination node, ξ_d.

The definition of the problem is from the high sequence-level perspective. The pragmatical implementation is based on the low node-level. To be more detailed, in an SDN network, given a pair of source and destination nodes for data transferring, there exist numerous paths connecting them. A adaptive way to find the optimal path is to ascertain one of the paths based on the current networking status to gain the maximal throughput that is identical to the definition in Chapter 5. Obviously, even given the identical source and destination pair, the solution is not always inclined to output the identical path attribute to the ever-changing states of networking.

6.4 Proposed Scheme

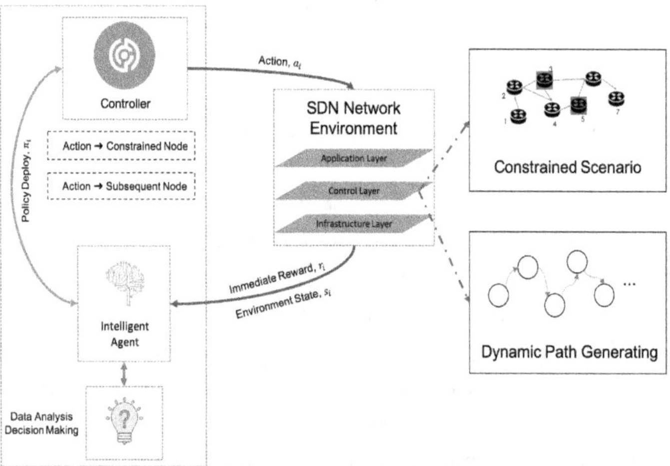

Fig. 6.2 Deep Reinforcement Learning in SDN Networking

Fig. 6.2 gives a clear illustration of Deep Reinforcement Learning paradigm proposed to integrate into the SDN network structure. From this framework, the close loop of Reinforcement learning fits well in centralized SDN networking. The entire SDN network is regarded as the object environment and returns key system statuses as environment observations. The intelligent agent collects the observed network data to approximate a global state and figures out the future movement based on the data. The agent is assigned into the controller to make the most of the SDN information collection mechanism. A series of decision making mechanisms and distributions comprise of the implicit policy that is deployed in the controller. The controller is the central pivot of the SDN network system, which can be embedded into the application layer as a high-hierarchical part or the controller layer as a low-level direct operator. Then the control imposes the actual influence on the network by taking an action based on the calculated policy. Once an action is implemented in the environment, a feedback signal, namely the immediate reward is produced to acknowledge the agent what performance networking is achieving. With the continuous feedback loop, the network system shall approach the optimal state and provide high quality services. As consequence, Fig. 6.2 genuinely instantiates the broadly-accepted framework in Fig. 6.1 with the SDN network platform and necessary modifications. Additionally, the two right-sided diagrams correspond to two scenarios, constrained path planning with performance optimization and dynamic path generating with optimal performance. Two different actions are also assigned to constrained nodes and subsequent nodes. The constrained scenario follows the idea of Chapter 5 but endeavors to search a particular node that enlarges throughput. The dynamic path generating follows the idea of dynamic routing in SDN environment to assign an optimal forwarding path for a request of interest. The action at time step i is denoted as a_i and r_i denotes instantly the returned reward from the environment, where $0 < i < \infty$. The policy π_i presented in Fig. 6.2 refers to a probability distribution $a_i = \pi_i = \pi(s_i)$ over all possible actions and the last step state. It is worth note that Fig. 6.2 represents the state as s_i at i step while in Fig. 6.1 denotes the state as observation, o_i.

For the optimization in the constrain condition, the Deep Q-learning is adopted here to dynamically discover the constrained node. Recall that the Deep Q-learning takes the action that maximizes the action-state Q value function, which is shown in Eq. 6.5 below. The discrepancy between the current expected value and the expected value of next state, plus an immediate reward is utilized as the update objective signal.

$$Q(s_i, a_i) = Q(s_i, a_i) + v[R_{i+1} + \gamma \max_a Q'(s_{i+1}, a_{i+1}) - Q(s_i, a_i)] \qquad (6.5)$$

In Eq. 6.5, v is the learning step size. From this rule, the Q-learning is inherently the off policy style that directs the Q-learning update to follow a fixed policy in greedy, $Q'(\cdot)$, instead of its own applied policy, $Q(\cdot)$. In this regard, $Q'(\cdot)$ is usually referred as a *target* policy and $Q(\cdot)$ is a *behavior* policy. In addition, the update paradigm belongs to the Temporal Difference (TD) class techniques, which are aware of an individual action along the expected estimation regardless of the actual sequence of actions in a complete experiment episode.

6.4.1 Constrained Path Planning

In order to accommodate the issue in the optimization in the constrain condition, two Q-learning policies, behavior policy and target policy, are set and built with two fully connected network models. In this situation, the environment state is extracted based on the switch port status query in SDN protocol, allowing the underlying physical switches in data plane to upload their ports status to the central controller in control plane. A significant measure is the ration of the actual network flow to the capacity of each link. Each link of a switch exactly corresponds to each neighbor. Hence, a mutual utilization ratio matrix can be constructed to reflect the transient data transferring state. The state for Deep Q-learning is thus defined as the port utilization ratio matrix retrieved by the port status. In the following, the reward is also based on a flow ratio while it is based on the actual deployed flow quantity and the expectation from configurations of the generator, as is defined in Eq. 6.6.

$$
R = \begin{cases} -\infty & \text{if the constrained path is invalid} \\ \log(\Delta_{real:expected}) & \text{if the constrained path is valid} \end{cases}
$$

$$
\Delta_{real:expected} = \frac{\rho_{real}}{\rho_{expected}}
$$

(6.6)

ρ_{real} is the real measured traffic and $\rho_{expected}$ denotes the ideal generated traffic. The constrained path depends on the constrain node. If the node causes a loop for networking transferring, the path selected is obviously invalid so that an extremely small reward (large penalty) is given. If the path is valid, the reward will be returned as described above.

6.4.2 Dynamic Node-level Prediction

For the other scenario, the optimization in the dynamic forwarding path planning, the fundamental Q-learning algorithm formation is similar except the update baseline. Theoretically, the Q-learning is a Temporal Difference (TD) off-policy method with one step ahead value evaluation and two asynchronous Q value models. The Temporal Difference with off-policy leads the learning process asymptotically to converging to the steady point. The problem is that it can be easily trapped into chasing error loop and fall into a sub-optimal area. On the contrary, the Monte Carlo control method collects a set of rewards based on the actual actions in episodes, with which the update error is towards the real experiment values instead of biased estimation. Though the Monte Carlo method requires suffers the high variance and slower than the Temporal Difference, as long as the adequate date are available, the Monte Carlo control can achieve competitive performance and reach the optimal results. The dynamic forwarding path planning faces more complex environment, larger state and action space, upon which the Monte Carlo control can guarantee the optimality.

Though the problem is defined as high sequence-level, in effect, the complete sequence is determined node-by-node from the source up to the destination. Therefore the state is then defined by the already inferred path. The action space is the node space in terms of the network topology. The reward is similar to the previous scenario based on the utilization and path validation. However, the node-level demands the path connectivity, indicating that each action selection can only take place in the neighbors of the latest action. In addition, the trail-and-error style episode sampling solely based on temporal port utilization is likely to cause performance damage to the convergence at the beginning, and even chaotic and unstable learning progress. As such, the transferring direction information is needed to seemingly *"drag"* the inference to the destination. At the last step of action sampling based on Q-values, the shortest path length is added, which indicates the path from each neighbor to the destination .

6.5 Experiments

To evaluate the feasibility of Reinforcement Learning, in this section, experiments are conducted with respect to two traffic engineering issues. The target network platform is the SDN-based architecture, with a control plane and a data switching plane. The constrained condition is evaluated on GEANT network topology and the dynamic path planning is testified on 10×10 Grid network topology, respectively. The learning machine platform is the same as Chapter 5. Fig. 6.3 shows a basic diagram of conducting experiments of constrained path planning. The data plane simulator is SDN-based network traffic simulator with a status reporting module, which will be described in the following. The control plane is based on POX SDN controller collecting port status as states to assist an intelligent agent. The intelligent agent is based on reinforcement learning to make decisions (take actions), namely choosing constrained nodes. The reward feedbacks are sent with port status to help the intelligent agent adjust the future actions. Similarly, the dynamic scenario in Fig. 6.4 is to deploy a traffic path into simulator by choosing forwarding hops one by one based on current state. The current state consists of the current switch node, its neighbors and the previous determined nodes segment. The reward here is given by the switch port bandwidth usage, which indicates whether there will be enough bandwidth for the demanded requests. In both cases, once a path is eventually implemented into the simulator, the throughput will be output as the target performance.

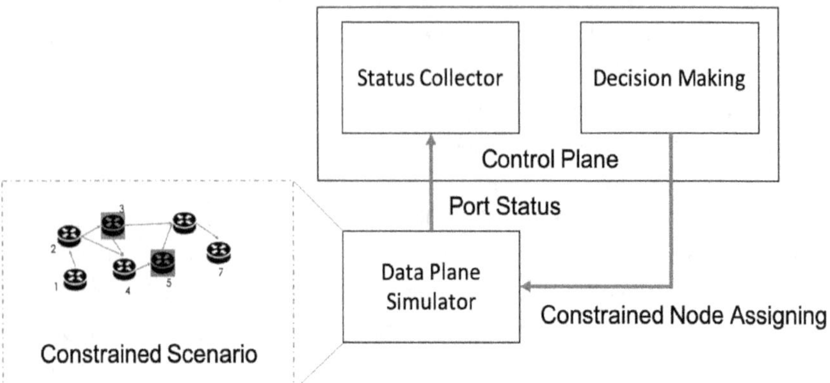

Fig. 6.3 The Experiment Diagram of Constrained Path Planning

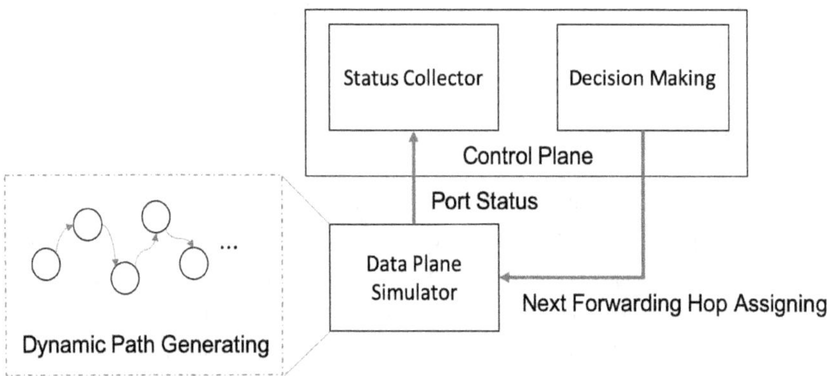

Fig. 6.4 The Experiment Diagram of Dynamic Path Planning

To perform the Reinforcement Learning process and the corresponding data sampling, a simple SDN-based network simulator is implemented. For the convenience and simplicity of experiments, the network simulator considers the active links between adjacent two nodes with exclusive flow occupation. That is a first-come-full-usage mode, which will allocate the the maximal transferring capacity to the foremost traffic requests and prevent the late requests when all the bandwidth resource is consumed. The purpose is to emphasize the limitation of link throughput capacity and make the control agent aware of the seriousness of busy path. Several key metrics will be directly calculated, such as the port utilization matrix and the corresponding rewards in light of the actions. The simulator finally returns the state, normalized rewards, episode end flag and a tuple containing any intriguing measures, which is inspired by a Reinforcement Learning simulator, *"gym"*, published by OpenAI [213]. To compare the throughput incrementation, a baseline of shortest path is added, which takes advantage of the Open Shortest Path First (OSPF) algorithm [214]. As default, the bandwidth of each link is 100 Mbps (12.5 MBps), and the traffic generation demand of each flow is 5 MBps. In the subsequent two sub-sections, the results and discussions are presented.

6.5.1   Evaluation of Constrained Path Planning

The experiment carried out here aims to gain the maximal throughput for all the data transferring requests under specific constrains similar to constrained traffic controlling in Chapter 5. To show feasibility of Deep Q-learning, one-node constrain control is evaluated and the specified node corresponds to the action in Markov Decision Process. Deep Q-learning model attempts to deliberately search a valid and high-return constrain in the action space for a given source-destination pair instead of random picking. In this experiment, total 20 requests will be executed in the simulator of the GEANT topology and a complete sampling episode consists of the entire length-20 simulation sequence.

As aforementioned, the state is defined as the current switch port status snapshot matrix. The state input plane of Deep neural network is thus a 5-layer fully connected neurons with the Relu activation function. The result is a Q-value vector with the same size as that of the action space. The other significant settings are: the discount factor γ being 0.99, the replay size being $2,000$, learning rate being 0.00001 and the batch size being 100.

Fig. 6.5 reveals a clear illustration that the throughput performance incrementally reaches its highest level and eventually converges at the relatively stable point. To be detailed, the green line is for the shortest path baseline, the orange one is the actual measure throughput and the red line refers to the moving average of the actual measure with $1,000$ steps. The one-node constrained path control gradually increases the overall throughput even from the very beginning of the experiment. Although it maintains the performance slightly below the baseline, the optimal solution has been achieved after nearly $20,000$ episodes without obvious reduction. The cause of being slight worse than the baseline is that the constrained path is likely to cause many traffic conflicts same as in Chapter 5. However, the overall performance is improved with the assistant of Deep Q-learning that explores the optimal option and exploit it to keep the state. The moving average of actual traffic measure shows the better results and offers a helpful improvement for traffic engineering.

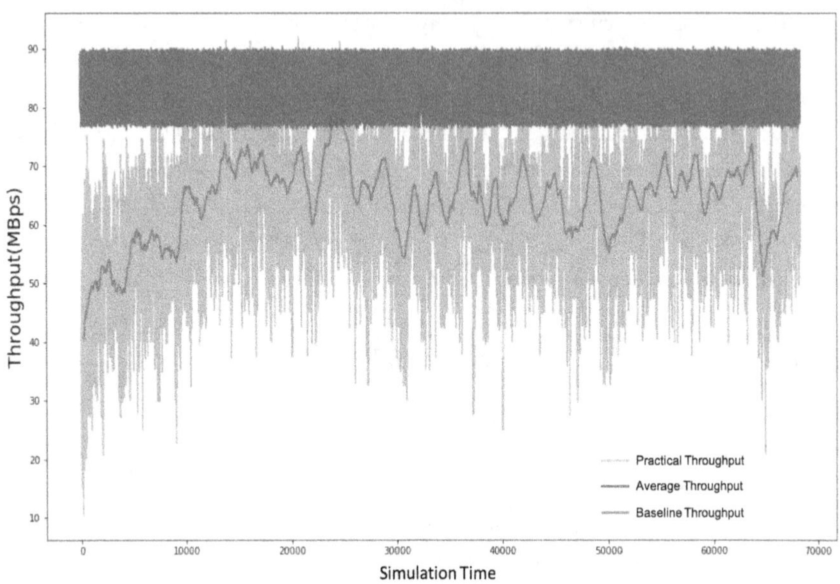

Fig. 6.5 The Throughput Gaining Based on One Node Constrained Path Planning

6.5.2 Evaluation of Dynamic Path Planning

In this part, an experiment is conducted with the similar traffic background in the 10×10 Grid network. 24 data transferring requests have been implemented as what is called imitated networking usage. With the settings of experiment environment, the target request is operational. The initial action is fixed as the source node and becomes the inferred sequential state in terms of the second taken action. Once the second action has been decided, the source node and the second node jointly become a previous inferred sequence for the third action, and so forth. The complete episode with respect to the Markov Decision Process ends when reaching the destination or a forwarding loop.

The sequential state is transformed by a 2-layer bi-directional LSTM block with 256 hidden state units, since it is required to be embedded as a computable distributed representation. Each action in a sequence is also embedded into an embedding space with embedding size being 256. To eliminate the temporal correlation along an episode, the experience replay is carried out with the memory size of 500,000. Other basic hyper-parameters are set as follows: the discount constant γ being 0.99, learning rate being 0.00001 and batch size being 500.

Fig. 6.6 illustrates the throughput achievement thanks to the dynamic path construction. The orange line is the actual traffic implemented by the dynamic learning algorithm and the

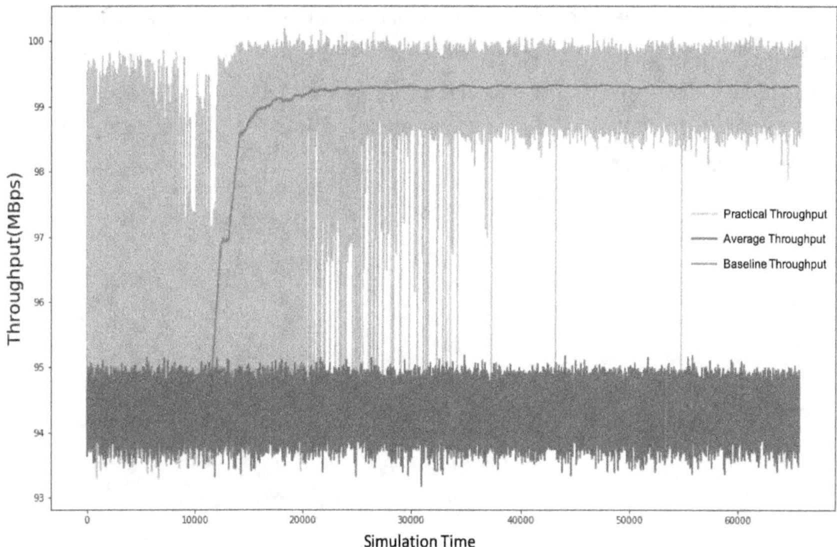

Fig. 6.6 The Throughput Gaining Based on Dynamic Forwarding Path Planning

red line is a moving average with $1,000$ steps. The dark green line is the OSPF baseline throughput. One simulation equals to one sampled episode. After around $10,000$ exploration in various available paths, the performance is stabilized after $20,000$ simulation because of the convergence of the learning agent. With more than $60,000$ simulations, the throughput has reached nearly 5 MBps more than the shortest path baseline with an apparent leap. The moving averaging reflects a trend on the whole regardless of possible errors and noise. The throughput is not a fixed value, ranging in 1.5 Mbps difference, since the implemented simulator added extra bandwidth reduction in each link to replay irresistible physical loss in the real world. The total trend remains steady without large fluctuation. It is able to draw a conclusion that the proposed Reinforcement Learning-based dynamic node-level predication adaptively promotes the network throughput performance and show promising direction of complex traffic engineering optimization.

6.6 Summary

In this Chapter, a Deep Q-learning based method is proposed for adaptive networking traffic engineering in two distinctive applications, constrained traffic control and dynamic forwarding path planning. The basic framework embedded in the SDN network is introduced along with the fundamentals of Reinforcement Learning process. It also presents the Q-learning in a well-defined mathematical formulation and its iterative update and learning method. The evaluation experiments conducted in terms of two scenarios in a dedicated simulator indicate that the Reinforcement Learning based technique advocates the decision agent to explore feasible solutions to achieve optimal points when facing highly complex networking environments.

Chapter 7

Conclusion and Future Work

The main contributions in this thesis concentrate on two aspects in intelligent networking management, fault management and performance management based on data mining and machine learning. The fault management part targets at anomaly and fault detection and localization in Micro-services architecture. The performance management part aims at network traffic engineering challenges and attempts to converge to optimal performance in terms of traffic throughput and transferring delay. The thesis outlines the main applicable scenarios and the analysis hierarchy in Chapter 1 and lists several challenges for effective management. An underlying idea throughout the thesis is the recent advances in machine learning shows a promising orientation for the automation and agile adaption of management and maintenance.

This Chapter summarizes the core techniques proposed and introduced in each previous chapters with empirical evaluations and their well-marked conclusions, followed by the next section for discussion of limitations and potential future research.

7.1   Conclusions

Fault and Anomaly Analysis:

For fault and anomaly analysis, two fundamental issues are presented: novelty identification with distributed representation; root cause localization with importance index and empirical errors.

The novelty identification successfully takes advantage of representative and compressed features embedded into a continuous space to reveal the hidden sample boundary. It is intriguing because the features are forged automatically as semantics of a task in terms of spatial-temporal information. The common wisdom assumes the features should be manually extracted from data with explicit meaning. However, a learning agent based on neural networks can encode sophisticated information into an implicit representative space. Especially, when it comes to log process, statistics-based algorithms prevail across academia and industry. Nevertheless, the representation learning for categorical logs shows another path to interpret implicit semantics in terms of systematic behaviors. Besides the embedding-like representation learning, the trace information is also significant for large-scale service-based architecture. The trace serves as a work-flow tracker of communications of intra-system services, which unfolds hierarchical and complicated linkage. The trace information has become an indispensable source for in-depth analysis.

As for the root cause localization, it makes the most of trace information not only to extract intrinsic importance index of involved services but also to investigate the servicing deviations against the normal baseline. The intrinsic importance index is constructed based on a query importance hypothesis. It is that one service is intuitively vital to its connected services if it is frequently queried by these neighbors. The hypothesis is similar to the PageRank method that works well in web page indexing. Additionally, the servicing deviations against the baseline come from the differences between empirical normal tasks and the tasks of interest with respect to durations of queries. The combination between intrinsic importance index and empirical errors will reasonably highlight suspicious nodes that may remain obscure under normal circumstances. The process even shows an opportunity to enable causality analysis for backtracking of root causes.

Data Driven Traffic Engineering Based on Learning

For traffic engineering, two ideas of supervised learning and reinforcement learning are presented respectively, traffic path planning with transferring constrains and optimizing network performance with constrains and dynamic forwarding.

The network traffic engineering relates to the allocation networking resource. A learning-based data-driven algorithm based on sequence-to-sequence is proposed to discover the hidden patterns entailed in the historical networking traffic data. The path planning process can be deemed as a transformation from traffic requests to available communication path allocation, which fit in a so-called *Encoder-Decoder* structure. The *Encoder-Decoder* structure helps project data from one domain into a latent space to keep common characteristics. It further projects the latent elements into target domain. Especially, recent successes in language processing show a promising direction to sequence-related analysis, for example network traffic engineering.

In the following dynamic traffic engineering scenario, it takes advantage of recent advances in Deep Reinforcement Learning to overcome the limitation of data labeling and unadaptive planning. This is because in real network environment, it is very difficult to collect labeled data and appoint the data to a corresponding downstream task. Generally, decision-making methods are required to be adaptive to dynamic surroundings. Reinforcement learning algorithms provide elastic searching policies to target at long term accumulated benefits and help gain global optimal performance. Despite the network complexity, reinforcement learning endeavors to reach a balance and trade-off between exploration and exploitation for optimization scheme so that reinforcement learning gives a promising result to tackle dynamic challenges.

7.2   Future Work

Network Data Representation Learning

The framework of network anomaly and fault detection takes heterogeneous data representation into consideration. The representation learning attempts to translate the data into computable metrics by various techniques stemming from other research areas, such as Natural Language Processing and image processing. It is then likely to bring system biases into networking analysis, since algorithms designed for other applications are not fully aware of the characteristics of networking analysis. Currently, there lack effective algorithms to interpret various data in the context of network properties and applications. For instance, several meta-configurations are vital to networking initial settings and conditions, but the recorded configurations can be stored in a variety of formats making it difficult to jointly wrap up. The unstructured topology data is traditionally denoted as a matrix, however the graph neural network [215, 216] improved by deep learning and graph theory shows exciting properties to comprehensively capture latent dependency. An informative and general representation with respective to networking applications will provide more insightful hidden information for in-depth analysis. It is worthwhile to have a deep investigation and review of existing representation learning trend and propose a reasonable approach to specifically capture the latent networking information.

Causality Analysis For Root Cause Tracking

In Chapter 4, the fault root cause localization is realized by the error degree with inherent systematic services importance based on the normal history baseline and PageRank index calculation. The idea emphasizes the most affected function point by the occurred faults, in other words the most suspicious localization. It is reasonable for clear hierarchical system structure, nevertheless the most affected node is not always the fault source in terms of a task. The dependency and connection between system components are very likely to amplify a tiny issue to a catastrophe via a long chain of fault propagation. Except propagation and amplification, tiny errors can accumulate continuous task by task and trigger a total failure explosion after long term latency. This type of errors can hardly be predicted as if they appeared as normal executions. It is therefore in an urgent need of causality analysis for an analyzer to trace back the fault source from terminal observation. As a matter of fact, causality analysis draws substantial attention to the artificial intelligence community [217–219] in spite of recent splendid advances in Deep Learning sphere. To reach the full automation and administrator-level diagnosis, the causality analysis enhanced by graph neural networks and deep learning gives a bright direction to reason about the latent root causes and localize ground truth fault sources.

Dynamic Network Traffic Engineering

It is manifest that supervised-based traffic path planning can achieve high performance but lack flexibility to adjust to novel situations. After sequence-to-sequence mode of planning, the processing for dynamic issues based on Deep Q-learning is further introduced and evaluated in terms of constrained conditions and individual node pre-diction. A potential approach to extend the availability of the algorithm is to combine sequence-to-sequence model and Reinforcement Learning. As aforementioned, the sequence-to-sequence model is preferable for paired source and target sequential data. The sequential processing mode is expected to be more efficient and inclined to circum-vent local optimums. In the presented evaluated experiments, the tested forwarding traffic data are somehow fixed and may cause over-fitting with respect to long term training. A feasible and useful solution is to generalize the Reinforcement Learning to massive environment background conditions, which will generate orders of magnitude more states and seemingly unstable background traffic occupation. In contrast to the research [10] that dedicates to flow allocation, node-level sequence finding offers adequate options and flexibility to accommodate seemingly chaotic environment states, and it can relieve the burden from re-training with respect to the latest data. Adjustable and node-level analysis will be a promising future work for intelligent network traffic engineering.

www.ingramcontent.com/pod-product-compliance
Lightning Source LLC
LaVergne TN
LVHW050651200726
843506LV00010B/1461